Lives of the Conjurers
Volume One

Lives of the Conjurers

Volume One

by Professor Solomon

Illustrated by Steve Solomon

TOP HAT PRESS
BALTIMORE

ISBN 978-0-912509-15-0

http://www.professorsolomon.com

Top Hat Press
Baltimore, Maryland

CONTENTS

Hocus Pocus

THE CONJURER KNOWN AS HOCUS POCUS IS A SHAD-
owy figure. He is mentioned in a work published
in 1656 by Thomas Ady, an English physician. Its
full title is *A Candle in the Dark: OR, A TREATISE Concern-
ing the Nature of Witches & Witchcraft: BEING Advice to
Judges, Sheriffes, Justices of the Peace and Grand-Jury-men,
what to do, before they passe Sentence on such as are
Arraigned for their Lives, as WITCHES.*

In his treatise Ady denounces the prosecution of persons
accused of witchcraft. He insists that there is no biblical
precedent for such prosecution. Even in ancient times, he
says, there were no witches or magicians with supernatural
powers—only practitioners of the "craft of Jugling [conjur-
ing]." These practitioners deceived the "silly people" who
beheld their trickery. They pretended to have "done great
Wonders, which were only delusions."

And he likens the wonder-workers of old to the conjurers
of his own day. Skill at deception "is profitably seen in our
common juglers, that go up and down to play their Tricks
in Fayrs and Markets." Ady then gives an example of these
itinerants: a conjurer known as Hocus Pocus.

> I will speak of one man more excelling in that craft than
> others, that went about in King *James* his time, and long
> since, who called himself, *The Kings Majesties most excellent
> Hocus Pocus,* and so was he called, because that at the play-
> ing of every Trick, he used to say, *Hocus pocus, tontus talon-
> tus, vade celeriter jubeo,* a dark composure of words, to
> blinde the eyes of the beholders, to make his Trick pass the
> more currantly without discovery, because when the eye
> and the ear of the beholder are both earnestly busied, the
> Trick is not so easily discovered, nor the Imposture dis-
> cerned; the going about of this Fellow was very useful to

the wise, to see how easily people among the ancient Heathen were deceived.

Thus, a treatise on witchcraft provides a brief description of a seventeenth-century conjurer. And while the conjurer's claim of royal patronage ("the Kings Majesties most excellent Hocus Pocus") sounds like puffery, it has in fact been confirmed—by the discovery of a royal warrant. In 1619 one William Vincent was granted a license "to exercise the art of Legerdemaine in any Townes within the Relme of England & Ireland." And who was William Vincent? In a court record from 1625, he is described as "alias Hocus Spocus, of London."*

Hocus Pocus was an author as well as a performer. In 1634 a pamphlet was published entitled *The Anatomie of LEGERDEMAIN, OR The Art of Jugling set forth in his proper colours, fully, plainly, and exactly, so that an ignorant person may thereby learn the full perfection of the same, after a little practise.* The author, identified as "Hocus Pocus Junior," is believed to have been Vincent.

The pamphlet contains instructions for tricks, in particular the Cups and Balls. And it lists the basic attributes of a conjurer:

> First, hee must be one of an impudent and audacious spirit, so that hee may set a good face upon the matter.
>
> Secondly, he must have a nimble and cleanly conveyance [i.e., his furtive moves must be light-fingered and adroit].
>
> Thirdly, he must have strange termes, and emphaticall words, to grace and adorn his actions, and the more to astonish the beholders.
>
> Fourthly, and lastly, such gesture of body as may leade away the spectators eyes from a strict and diligent beholding his manner of conveyance.

---

* The record was of a legal proceeding in Leicester. Vincent (Hocus Pocus) was accused of having cheated another player in a game of backgammon. He denied the charge, and seems to have escaped punishment.

Surely a description of Hocus Pocus himself!

In 1647 the poet John Cleveland published these lines, referring apparently to one of Hocus's tricks:

> Before a *Scot* can properly be curst,
> I must (like Hocus) swallow daggers first.

And finally, an epitaph for him is found in the miscellany *Wit's Recreations* (1650):

On Hocas Pocas

Here *Hocas* lyes with his tricks and his knocks,
Whom death hath made sure as a juglers box;
Who many hath cozen'd by his leiger-demain,
Is presto convey'd and here underlain.
Thus *Hocas* he's here, and here he is not,
While death plaid the *Hocas,* and brought him
   to th'pot [grave].

For Death too is a conjurer. He had waved his wand and intoned "strange termes." And presto! Hocus was conveyed to the Grave.

The Famous Mr. Fawkes

BARTHOLOMEW FAIR WAS BOTH A TRADE EVENT, FOR cloth and other commodities, and a carnival. Held each summer at West Smithfield, in north-west London, it lasted four days and drew large crowds. A variety of entertainment was offered. There were acrobats, puppeteers, musicians, fire-eaters, wild animals, peep shows and mechanical rides. And there were conjurers—or jugglers, as they were then called. The most popular of these was a performer known as Fawkes.*

Fawkes performed in an enclosed theatrical booth. Half-a-dozen shows were presented daily. A banner outside the booth depicted Fawkes—dressed like a gentleman, in a powdered wig—producing eggs from his Egg Bag. And there was more to the show than the celebrated Egg Bag—as promised by an ad that appeared in newspapers:

> THIS is to give Notice, That the famous Mr. FAWKS at his Booth in West-Smithfield, performs the following most surprizing Tricks, after a new Method, viz. He takes an empty Bag, lays it on the Table, and turns it several Times inside out, then commands 100 Eggs out of it, and several Showers of real Gold and Silver; then the Bag beginning to swell, several Sorts of wild Fowl run out of it upon the Table. He throws up a Pack of Cards, and causes them to be living Birds flying about the Room. He causes living Beasts, Birds, and other Creatures to appear upon the

---

* His full name remained unknown until Houdini—researching a book on the history of magic—set out to learn it. Houdini and the clerk of St. Martin-in-the-Fields Church searched through the parish records, and found the will of Isaac Fawkes. He had died in 1731, and had bequeathed a sizeable sum—earned as a conjurer—to his wife.

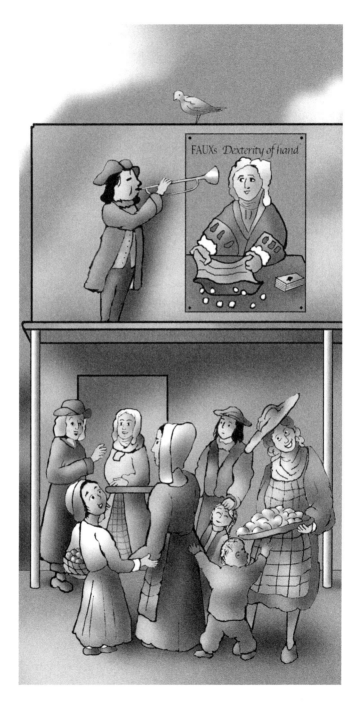

Table. He blows the Spots of the Cards off or on, and changes them to any pictures.

Fawkes was a pioneer of advertising; and newspaper notices such as this, along with his handbills and broadsides, drew a steady stream of patrons. He set up his booth at fairs—offering "curiosities no person in the Kingdom can pretend to show like himself"—and prospered. The *London Journal* reported:

> The Famous Mr Fawks, as he modestly stiles himself, has since Bartholomew and Southwark-Fairs, put seven hundred Pounds into the Bank: He may certainly challenge any Conjurer of the Age to do the like.

His popularity at fairs allowed him to move on to theatres. Beginning in 1725, he performed regularly at the Old Tennis Court playhouse, which became known at Fawkes' Theatre. His show now included mechanical wonders—automata built by Christopher Pinchbeck, a clock-maker with whom he had become partners. Increasingly, Pinchbeck's automata and other creations were featured. Among them was a "Musical Clock, that plays Variety of Tunes, on Organ, Flute and Flageolet; with birds Whistling and Singing as Natural as Life itself."

That Fawkes was both a savvy showman and a masterful performer is evidenced by an article that appeared in the *Weekly Journal.* The writer describes his reception at the theatre:

> I was tempted the other Day to go and see the Performance of the famous and learned Mr FAWKES, the famous Master in *Legerdemain.* He is a Person of singular good Breeding, for knowing me to be a Virtuoso, he caused the Door keeper to return me my Money, and at the same Time complimented me with the Liberty of the House....It put me into a high good Humour to find that Mr *Fawkes* understood himself so well, and made me relish his Entertainment the better.

And he tells how Fawkes opened the show:

> What *Lucien* tells of one *Pancrates,* a Magician of *Egypt,* is much of the same nature with what we see him [Fawkes] do. It seems, whenever *Pancrates* travell'd it was his custom, as soon as he came into his Inn, with his Magick Wand to touch the first Log of Wood he found, and pronouncing certain unintelligible Syllables over it, it immediately became a Man, and ready to obey his Commands. . . . I perceive that Mr *Fawkes* follows *Pancrates* in the Exercise of the *Wand,* and that before he begins any *Transformations,* he whispers the Wand, to the great Amazement and Terror of the Spectators.*

Fawkes was also available for private performances, at the theatre or in the homes of the well-to-do. (On one occasion he entertained the future George II.) And he offered "to learn any Gentlemen and Ladies his Fancies by Dexterity of Hand for their own Diversion." Magic lessons from the master!

Little is known of his personal life. He had a son who took part in the show, performing as a contortionist. And he was religious. His will, composed on his death-bed, begins:

> *In the name of God Amen*
>
> I, Isaac Fawkes, of the Parish of St. Martin-in-the-Fields, of the Liberty of Westminster, being sick and weak in body but of sound mind and memory, thanks be given to Almighty God for the same, and calling to mind and duly considering the uncertainty of this mortal life and that it is appointed unto all men once to die, do make and ordain this to be my Last Will and Testament. First and principally I commit my soul into the hands of my Dear Redeemer and my body to the earth to be decently buried.

---

* The anonymous author of this article may have been Daniel Defoe, who was writing for the *Weekly Journal* at the time.

He goes on to bequeath his assets—in excess of 10,000 pounds—to "my truly and well beloved wife, Alice Fawkes."

In earlier times, conjurers (along with actors, ballad-singers, and other "vagabonds") had been viewed by the authorities with suspicion. In some places, they were even suspected of witchcraft. Fawkes was the first of his profession to achieve respectability—or at least fame and fortune.

The Bottle Conjurer

O N THE EVENING OF JANUARY 16, 1749, AN EXPECTANT crowd had filled a theater in London. Among those waiting for the show to begin were the Duke of Cumberland—brother of the king—and others of high rank. What had drawn this crowd was an advertisement that had appeared in the newspapers:

> AT THE NEW THEATRE IN THE HAYMARKET, on Monday next…is to be seen a Person who performs the several most surprising things following,—viz., 1st. He takes a common walking Cane from any of the Spectators, and thereupon plays the music of every Instrument now in use, and likewise sings to surprising perfection. 2dly. He presents you with a common Wine Bottle, which any of the spectators may first examine; this Bottle is placed on a Table in the middle of the Stage, and he (without any equivocation) goes into it, in the sight of all the Spectators, and sings in it; during his stay in the bottle, any Person may handle it, and see plainly that it does not exceed a common Tavern Bottle.
>
> Those on the Stage, or in the Boxes, may come in masked habits (if agreeable to them); and the performer, if desired, will inform them who they are.
>
> Stage, 7s. 6d. Boxes, 5s. Pit, 3s. Gallery, 2s. To begin a half an hour after six o'clock.
>
> Tickets to be had at the Theatre.
>
> The performance continues about two hours and a half.

But when the performance failed to take place, a riot ensued. A newspaper account of it appeared the next day:

> Last night (viz. *Monday* the 16th), the much expected drama of "The Bottle Conjurer," at the *New theatre* in the *Haymarket,* ended in the tragi-comical manner following.

Curiosity had drawn together prodigious numbers. About seven, the Theatre being lighted up, without so much as a single fiddle to keep the audience in good humour, many grew impatient. Immediately followed a chorus of catcalls, heightened by loud vociferations, and beating with sticks; when a fellow came from behind the curtain, and bowing, said, that if the performer did not appear, the money should be returned; at the same time a wag crying out from the pit, that if the ladies and gentlemen would give double prices the conjurer would get into a pint bottle. Presently a young gentleman in one of the boxes seized a lighted candle and threw it on the stage. This served as the charge for sounding to battle. Upon this the greater part of the audience made the best of their way out of the Theatre; some losing a cloak, others a hat, others a wig, and swords also. One party, however, staid in the house, in order to demolish the inside… they tore up the benches, broke to pieces the scenes, pulled down the boxes; in short dismantled the Theatre entirely, carrying away the particulars above mentioned into the street, where they made a mighty bonfire; the curtain being hoisted on a pole, by way of a flag. A large party of guards were sent for, but came time enough only to warm themselves round the fire.

The promise of a refund was never honored, the box-office receipts having vanished during the melee. (Some claimed that the conjurer had indeed appeared, and had made off with the proceeds.) Also missing was the Duke of Cumberland's sword. Angered by the non-appearance of the conjurer, Cumberland had stood up in his box, waved his drawn sword, and called for the house to be pulled down—helping to incite the riot. During the disorder, someone had wrested the sword from his grasp. A reward of 30 guineas was offered for its return.

Who was responsible for the advertisement? According to the theatre owner, a strange man had arranged to rent the theatre on behalf of the conjurer. But clearly, the whole thing had been a hoax. And years later, it was learned that the Duke of Montagu and his friends had concocted it. It seems they had been discussing the question of human gullibility.

"I will wager," said Montagu, "that let a man advertise the most impossible thing in the world, he will find fools enough in London to fill a playhouse and pay handsomely for the privilege of being there."

"Surely," said Lord Chesterfield, "if a man should say that he would jump into a quart bottle, nobody would believe that."

To settle the wager, these noblemen rented a theatre, composed the advertisement, and placed it in newspapers.

Montagu won his wager. There was standing-room only that night, to watch the conjurer jump into a bottle.*

---

* In *Games of Skill and Conjuring,* published anonymously in 1861, are found these instructions for performing a trick called "The Bottle Conjuror": "You must preface this trick by declaring to the company that it was formerly supposed to be impossible to set the Thames on fire, and that it was demonstrated some years ago at the Haymarket Theatre, that for a person to crawl into a quart bottle was an utter impossibility, but since then the progress made in all kinds of knowledge has proved it is possible to set the Thames on fire, and that any one may crawl *in to* a pint bottle. This statement will of course be doubted, and to prove your assertion, get a pint bottle and place it in the middle of the room; then slip outside the door, and in a minute or two return, creeping upon all-fours, saying: 'Ladies and gentlemen, this is crawling *in to* the pint bottle!'"

Cagliostro

THE MAN KNOWN AS THE COUNT DE CAGLIOSTRO DIED in a dungeon—a solitary cell in the Castle of San Leo. He had been imprisoned by the Inquisition for the crime of heresy.

A century later, Henry Ridgely Evans was in Paris, and attended a performance by a latter-day Cagliostro:

In the summer of 1893, a conjurer calling himself "Cagliostro" was astonishing Paris with his feats of fin-de-siècle magic. Being a student of occultism generally, but more particularly of natural magic and legerdemain, I went to see the nineteenth-century necromancer exhibit his marvels. I saw some very clever illusions performed during the evening, but nothing that excited my especial interest as a devotee of the weird and wonderful, until the prestidigitator came to his pièce de résistance—the Mask of Balsamo.

The conjurer brought out a mask—a waxen face resembling a death-mask. Descending from the stage, he passed it about for examination. Then he placed the mask on a small, undraped table in the center aisle of the theatre.

"Messieurs et mesdames," said the professor of magic and mystery, "this mask is a perfect likeness of Joseph Balsamo, Count de Cagliostro, the famous sorcerer of the eighteenth century. It is a reproduction of a death-mask which is contained in the secret museum of the Vatican at Rome. Behold! I lay the mask upon this table in your midst. Ask any question you will of Balsamo, and he will respond."

The mask rocked to and fro with weird effect at the bidding of the conjurer, rapping out frequent answers to queries put by the spectators.

An amateur magician, Evans was not mystified by the rappings of the mask; he knew them to be a mere electrical trick. (An electromagnet was powered via wires inside a leg of the table.) But he was intrigued by the mask itself. Was it truly a likeness of the Count de Cagliostro, the wonder-worker whose séances had mystified the court of Louis XVI?

Returning to his hotel, Evans found himself bewitched by the mask. "I was pursued all the next day, and for weeks afterward, with visions of the enchanter." His curiosity roused, he searched the bookstalls along the Seine. Finally, he found a biography—a brief work titled *Vie de Joseph Balsamo, connu sous le nom de Comte Cagliostro.*

> The frontispiece was an engraved portrait of Cagliostro. Yes, here was the great magician staring at me from out the musty, faded pages of a quaint old chronicle. A world of cunning lay revealed in the depths of his bold, gleaming eyes. His thick lips wore a smile of Luciferian subtlety.

Who exactly was Cagliostro? Who was this mystery man —this alchemist, healer, prognosticator, medium, founder of Egyptian Masonry, and conjurer—this portly "Prince of Quacks," as Carlyle called him—who became the idol of Paris in the years just before the Revolution? Who was the original of the Mask of Balsamo?

Was he purely a charlatan, as his enemies insisted (and as history has painted him)? Or was he—at least in part— what he claimed to be? Behind the veil of mystery that masked his identity, who was Alessandro de Cagliostro?

●

Of his origins and early years, there are two versions. The first is found in that biography that Evans brought back to his hotel room. Published in 1790 by the office of the Inquisition, *Vie de Joseph Balsamo* was based on a series of newspaper articles, written by a journalist in the pay of his enemies and intended to discredit him. It claims that

"Count Cagliostro" was actually Joseph Balsamo, a low-born Sicilian adventurer. Balsamo's criminal history, and his dissolute ways, are recounted in detail.

Cagliostro denied being Balsamo. And there was no evidence that he was—only the assertion of a corrupt journalist. Moreover, the characters of the two men were dissimilar. The contrast was striking, as Evans points out:

> Balsamo was devoid of education, or even the appearance of respectability; grasping, scheming, and utterly disreputable. Comte de Cagliostro was a highly accomplished man; a chemist of no mean ability; an empiric, who made many remarkable cures of diseases that baffled the medicos of the period; a psychic and a mesmerizer.... As Trowbridge [a later biographer] says: "Whoever Cagliostro may have been, he could certainly never have been Joseph Balsamo."

Yet no more credible is Cagliostro's own version of his past. His original name (according to his testimony in the Affair of the Diamond Necklace) was Acharat. He was the child of noble parents, he claimed. Born in Malta and orphaned at a young age, he wound up in Arabia, where he was raised in the palace of the Great Muphti. During his youth an adept named Althotas tutored him in the occult sciences, and took him on a tour of the East. While in Egypt Acharat received instruction in ancient mysteries—from the High Priest himself! And it was upon this knowledge that he would base his reforms of Masonry. Finally, he bid farewell to Althotas and returned to Malta. And adopting the name Cagliostro, he became an alchemist.

Or at least, that is the tale he told. But it is not until Cagliostro arrived in London in 1776—accompanied by his wife Seraphina, the "Countess de Cagliostro"—that his story becomes historical. While in London he is known to have practiced alchemy, in a laboratory-residence on Whitcombe street. He dispensed medicinal concoctions. And he was inducted into a Masonic lodge that met at the King's Head tavern in Soho.

But after two years in London, Cagliostro fled the city. Having lost most of his money to swindlers, he had developed legal problems and feared imprisonment. Along with Seraphina, he began to wander from city to city in Europe. As he did so, his reputation as an alchemist, healer, and wonder-worker began to grow.

To be sure, there were set-backs along the way—in particular, during his stay in Warsaw. He had been welcomed by Prince Poninsky and given lodging in the palace. There he concocted his medicines and prescribed them for ailments. He also conducted séances, whose purpose was both to communicate with the unseen world and to entertain. But they were less than successful. Evans reports:

> He chose as his clairvoyant a little girl, eight years of age. After pouring oil into her hands, he closed her in a room, the door of which was hung with a black curtain. The spectators sat outside. He interrogated the child concerning the visions that appeared to her. Among other tests, he requested the spectators to inscribe their names on a piece of paper which he appeared to burn before their very eyes. Calling to the child that a note would flutter down at her feet, he requested her to pass it to him through the door....[It] contained the signatures of the spectators. This was nothing more than the trick of a prestidigitateur, such as was performed by Philadelphia and Pinetti, the two great sleight of hand artists of the period. The next day the clairvoyant confessed the fact that she had been tutored by the magician, and that the visions were but figments of the imagination.

On another occasion, Cagliostro—amid clouds of incense on a dimly-lit stage—summoned the spirit of the High Priest of Egypt. He left the stage; and after a moment the High Priest, bearded and garbed in a robe and a turban, emerged from the darkness.

"What see ye?" he asked the spectators.

"I see," replied a skeptical member of the audience, "that

Monsieur le Comte de Cagliostro has disguised himself with a mask and a full white beard."

With a wave of his hands the High Priest extinguished the two candles on the stage. The sound of a robe being slipped off was distinctly heard. When the candles were relit, the High Priest was gone—and Cagliostro had returned to the stage.

And there was a final embarrassment in Warsaw. In the laboratory of a local alchemist, Cagliostro demonstrated the transmutation of mercury into silver:

> Girt with a freemason's apron, and standing on a black floor marked with cabalistic symbols in chalk, Cagliostro worked at the furnace. In the gloom of twilight the proceedings were held. By a clever substitution of crucibles, Cagliostro apparently accomplished the feat of transmutation, but the fraud was detected the next morning, when one of the servants of the house discovered the original crucible containing the mercury, which had been cast upon a pile of rubbish by the pretended alchemist, or one of his confederates.

It was time to move on. The Cagliostros packed their bags, called for their coach, and departed. (According to one report, they "decamped during the night.") Three months later, in September 1780, the Count and Countess turned up in Strasburg. And it was there that Cagliostro's career took a favorable turn. After performing numerous healings (at no charge) for the populace, he drew the attention—and financial support—of Cardinal Rohan. Enormously rich, Rohan enjoyed a life of luxury in his villa at Strasburg. He was impressed by Cagliostro's healings, psychic powers, and alchemical expertise—in particular the last. For Rohan was passionate about alchemy, and maintained a well-equipped laboratory at his villa.

Given free use of the laboratory, Cagliostro conducted alchemical experiments and was reputed to have achieved astonishing results. But since his arrival, skeptics had questioned the genuineness of his wonders. Among them was the Baroness d'Oberkirch, one of the grand ladies of Strasburg. Visiting the Cardinal one day, she expressed her view that Count Cagliostro was a charlatan. Insisting otherwise, Rohan showed her the diamond ring on his little finger.

"A beautiful gem, monseigneur," said the Baroness. "I have been admiring it."

"Well, it was Cagliostro who made it: he made it out of nothing! I was present during the whole operation, with my eyes fixed on the crucible. Is that not science, Baroness?"

Baroness d'Oberkirch (had she known the adage) might have argued that the hand is quicker than the eye.

Some time later, Cagliostro sought to convince the Baroness that his psychic powers were real. Gazing at her intently, he told her that she was an only child and had lost her mother long ago. The Baroness was not impressed: he could easily have learned these facts. Nonetheless, she was impressed by Cagliostro's *gaze*. "He was not, strictly speaking, handsome," she recalls in her memoirs. "But never have I seen a more remarkable face. His glance was so penetrating that one might almost be tempted to call it supernatural....a mix of fire and ice."

Cagliostro stayed in Strasburg for three years. He remained a favorite of the Cardinal, who—never doubting his powers—provided him with ample funds and even loaned him a villa. (It was dubbed "Cagliostrano.") But the Count grew restless. And in 1783 he and the Countess moved on to Bordeaux, and then to Lyons.

Cagliostro had become an avid participant in Masonry; and during his travels he had been promoting a reformed version of it. The Rite of Egyptian Masonry, as he called it, was his own creation. It was based, he claimed, on arcane knowledge he had acquired in Egypt. (More likely, it derived from a book by an obscure mystic named George Coston.) The Egyptian Rite was a blend of Masonry and occultism. Its stated aim was the spiritual redemption of mankind. According to Cagliostro, Masonry had lost touch with its original spirituality—a quality that his Rite would restore. In addition, adherents were promised prolonged life (via an elixir); wealth (gold would be created alchemically); and communion with the spirit world (during the séances that he conducted).

While in Strasburg, Cagliostro had founded a lodge of Egyptian Masonry; and it had attracted a few followers. But it was in Lyons—a stronghold of Masonry—that his Rite found enthusiastic support. Men and women alike were invited to participate. Initiations were held; funds were raised; and a temple was built. It was designated the Lodge of Triumphant Wisdom. And its High Priest, or Grand Cophta, was Cagliostro.

Meanwhile, he had remained in touch with Cardinal Rohan, who was residing now in Paris. And when the prelate invited him to come and demonstrate his wonders to Parisians, Cagliostro did not hesitate. Traveling to Paris in his four-horse coach, he moved into a house the Cardinal had found for him; set up a laboratory; and began his stay in the city. He would remain there for nearly two years— the last nine months spent as a prisoner in the Bastille.

His popularity in Paris was immediate and phenomenal. Like Mesmer before him, Count Cagliostro became a sensation. "The Friend of Mankind," as he called himself, was much discussed; and portraits of the bewigged alchemist were everywhere—on prints, fans, snuff-boxes. There was even a Cagliostro hat! For the afflicted he performed healings, at no charge. For Masons he established a lodge of the Egyptian Rite. And for those who could afford them, his séances became the latest rage. Idle aristocrats flocked to his house on the rue St.-Claude—for an encounter with the spirits of the dead.

A theatrical experience awaited them. Arriving at the house, these guests were led to the second floor by servants dressed as Egyptian slaves. Passing through a richly-furnished apartment, they entered the séance room, or *chambre égyptienne*. It was hung with drapery and dimly lit by candles in tall sconces. The walls were lined with statues of Egyptian gods. On a table was a large globe of water. The guests sat themselves at the table and awaited their host.

And in he came—the Grand Cophta! Cagliostro wore a black robe, embroidered with hieroglyphics, and a turban ornamented with jewels. Taking his place at the table, he talked about the occult. And he was an eloquent speaker. According to Count Beugnot (a genuine count): "If gibberish can be sublime, Cagliostro was sublime. When he began any subject he seemed carried away with it, and spoke impressively in a ringing, sonorous voice."

Finally, a boy was brought in, hypnotized, and told to gaze into the globe of water. And he was able to glimpse therein the spirits of the dead. Guests would request the spirit of some historical personage. Cagliostro then evoked that spirit; and the boy described the figure that appeared. Gazing into the globe, he was also able to discern future events.

How genuine were these demonstrations? Did spirits of the dead actually visit the *chambre égyptienne*? Did the boy glimpse them in the globe, or was it all a charade—pseudomysticism designed to dupe the credulous? That is to say, was Cagliostro indeed a charlatan?

Opinions have varied. The standard view is that he was a fraud. But W. R. H. Trowbridge, author of *Cagliostro: The Splendour and Misery of a Master of Magic* (1910), deems him to have been authentic—a bona fide alchemist, occultist, and healer who, admittedly, resorted on occasion to trickery: "To attract followers, he was no longer content to gratify the passion for the marvelous, but sought to stimulate it. To enhance the effect of his phenomena he had recourse to artifices worthy of a mountebank."

"Ordinary conjuring tricks," concludes Trowbridge, "were undoubtedly employed."

Henry Ridgely Evans held a similar view: "That he made use, at times, of natural means to accomplish his wonders, such as the instruments of conjuring and phantasmagoria, with all the effective *mise-en-scène* of lights, draperies, Egyptian and Rosicrucian emblems, etc., may be admitted; but that does not detract from his undoubted gifts as a genuine psychic."

To be sure, his descendants were the *totally* fake mediums of the nineteenth and twentieth centuries. "He did not disdain to use the methods of a Pinetti or a Philadelphia to enhance his mystical séances," says Evans. "He claimed to be able to evoke the spirits of the dead. In fact, he was the prototype of the modern spirit medium."

Yet Cagliostro must be given his due, Evans insists. "Charlatan or no charlatan, he was one of the most fascinating characters of his time."

And indeed he was. Soon after his arrival in the city, all of Paris was talking about him. "The admiration and curiosity that Cagliostro aroused in all classes of society," says Trowbridge, "reached a degree of infatuation little short of idolatry." Many joined his lodge of Egyptian Masonry, paying the sizeable membership fee. The sick came to him for healing. The well-to-do paid to attend his séances. Cagliostro's celebrity soared; and his coffers filled.

But on the morning of August 22, 1785, his success came to an end. The police came to his house, arrested him, and laying hold of him by the collar, led him through the streets. Their destination was the Bastille. For he had been implicated in the Affair of the Diamond Necklace.

Cardinal Rohan too had been arrested and taken to the Bastille (though unlike Cagliostro, the prelate was given a luxurious suite within the prison). Both men had been accused—falsely—of complicity in an elaborate swindle, involving a necklace. Their arrests had been demanded by Queen Marie-Antoinette. For her own integrity had been impugned by the affair (in which a prostitute had impersonated her); and the Queen was furious.

Cagliostro was imprisoned for nine months, awaiting trial. In the end, both he and Rohan were acquitted and set free. As Cagliostro returned home, thousands came out to cheer him. For unlike Marie-Antoinette, he was a popular figure in Paris.

His acquittal, however, was an embarrassment for the Queen. And the next day Cagliostro was banished from

France. He was given one week in which to leave Paris, and three weeks in which to be gone from the country.

So the Count and Countess hastily packed their bags and made their way to London. The day after arriving, Cagliostro wrote his famous *Lettre au peuple français.* It was a denunciation of the government that had wrongly imprisoned and then exiled him. Published as a pamphlet, it was widely read in France and "created an immense sensation," says Trowbridge. "It assailed more or less openly the monarchical principle itself. Of all the pamphlets which from the Necklace Affair to the fall of the Bastille attacked the royal authority none are so dignified or so eloquent." In addition, his lawyers in Paris filed a lawsuit, against the chief of police and the governor of the Bastille.

In response, a campaign was launched—by a hireling of the French government—to blacken his name and ruin him. A series of articles defaming Cagliostro appeared in a London newspaper. They quoted false testimony regarding his past, and accused him of being a charlatan, an impostor, the scoundrel Balsamo. At the same time, a legal persecution was orchestrated. Spurious creditors began to descend on Cagliostro. These individuals had been secretly paid to take out writs against him for non-existent debts. To add to his misery, local Masons had turned against him, rejecting and mocking the Egyptian Rite.

In the end Cagliostro was forced to flee London—once again—to avoid being sent to debtor's prison. He and Seraphina now began several years of wandering about Europe. A decade earlier, they had been welcome guests in the cities they visited; but such was no longer the case. The libels against Cagliostro had been widely circulated, as had his pamphlet expressing anti-monarchical sentiments. Local authorities looked upon him now as a fraud, and as a troublemaker who espoused the revolutionary spirit that was afoot in France. In Turin, for example, no sooner had he entered the town than he was told to leave. Trowbridge paints a bleak picture of these years:

The luxury and flattery so dear to him were gone for ever. His journeys from place to place were no longer triumphal processions but flights. Dishonoured, discredited, disillusioned, the once superb High Priest of the Egyptian Mysteries, the "divine Cagliostro," accustomed to be courted by the greatest personages, acclaimed by the crowd, and worshipped by his adherents, was now shadowed by the police, shunned wherever he was recognized, hunted from pillar to post. All towns in which he was likely to be known were carefully avoided; into such as seemed to offer a chance of concealment he crept stealthily. He dared not show his face anywhere.

Cagliostro was "bankrupt in reputation, in purse, and in friends." He ended up in Rome, "into which he crawled like a beast wounded to the death that has just enough strength to reach its lair." Seraphina had family there; and the connection may have drawn them to the city. But Cagliostro seemed drawn to his doom as well. For the Papal authorities had pronounced Masonry to be heretical and seditious, and its practice to be a capital offense. Yet while living in Rome, he sought recruits for his Egyptian Rite.

The authorities got wind of these efforts; and in December 1789, Cagliostro was arrested. He was accused of being a Mason, a heretic, a revolutionary agent, and an enemy of the Church. Tried in a court of the Inquisition, he was found guilty and sentenced to death; but the sentence was commuted to life imprisonment. All of the papers that had been found in his possession, including the manuscript for a book on Egyptian Masonry, were burnt.

Cagliostro was taken to the Castle of San Leo. "The situation of this stronghold," says Trowbridge, "is one of the most singular in Europe. The enormous rock, whose summit it crowns, rising on three sides precipitously from an almost desert plain, is like a monument commemorative of some primeval convulsion of nature." His cell in the tower had a small window, through which was visible the village below. On the wall was a crucifix. A priest came to him daily, for confession.

At times he was subject to rages. Cagliostro would shake the bars on the window, shout prophecies, curse the guards, or even howl like a madman. At other times he claimed to be penitent, and made lengthy confessions—although his jailers doubted his sincerity. Tormented by his confinement, he became a pathetic figure. In the end he may even have lost his mind.

In 1797 forces from revolutionary France captured San Leo, and inquired if Cagliostro, whom they regarded as an apostle of liberty, was living. They wanted to free him. But he had died a year ago, they were told, and was buried in an unmarked grave.

●

Upon returning home from France, Henry Ridgely Evans remained fascinated by Cagliostro. He gathered information about him, wrote articles, and eventually published a book: *Cagliostro and His Egyptian Rite of Freemasonry* (1919). And he learned that Cagliostro's house still existed, and that it had a story of its own:

> The sombre old mansion has had a peculiar history. Cagliostro locked the doors of the laboratories and séance-chambre some time in June, 1786, on the occasion of his exile from France. All during the great Revolution the house remained closed and intact. Twenty-four years of undisturbed repose passed away. The dust settled thick upon everything; spiders built their webs upon the gilded ceilings of the salons. Finally, in the Napoleonic year 1810, the doors of the temple of magic and mystery were unfastened, and the furniture and rare curios, the retorts and crucibles, belonging to the dead conjurer, were auctioned off. An idle crowd of curious *quid nuncs* [busybodies] gathered to witness the sale and pry about.*

---

* Evans was told by one of his correspondents in Paris: "The sale took place in the apartment which he had occupied, and was con-

Eventually, the house was divided up into individual units. The tenants included a watchmaker, a feather curler, and a manufacturer of cardboard boxes. Its original inhabitant—once the idol of Paris—was forgotten.

> People pass and repass this ghost-house of the Rue Saint Claude every day but not one in a hundred knows that the great enchanter once resided there, and held high court. If those dumb walls could but speak, what fascinating stories of superstition and folly they might unfold to our wondering ears! Yes, in this ancient house, dating back to pre-Revolutionary Paris, to the old régime, the great necromancer known as Cagliostro lived, in the zenith of his fame.

In the summer of 1908, Evans returned to France and made a pilgrimage to the house. "The gloomy old mansion of the Rue Saint Claude affected me strangely," he says. Crossing its courtyard, he passed through a portal and climbed a stone staircase. On the second floor he peered into what had been the *chambre égyptienne*—now the workshop of a furniture maker. A young worker was upholstering a chair.

Exploring further, Evans climbed up to the attic. He looked down into the courtyard, "half expecting every minute, in my excited imagination, to see the gilded coach of the Cardinal de Rohan come rolling up to the doorway, and the Cardinal, in his splendid court costume, alight." And he tells of making a hasty departure:

> I slowly descended the ghost-haunted, time-worn staircase, feeling my way carefully along in the semi-darkness, and holding on to the forged-iron balustrade, thinking all

---

ducted by order of the municipal government. An examination revealed many curious acoustical and optical arrangements constructed in the building by Cagliostro. By the aid of these contrivances and that of well-trained confederates, he perpetrated many supposedly magical effects, summoned the shades of the dead."

the while of the high-born seigneurs and ladies who once passed up and down that winding way. I could almost hear the *frou-frou* of their silken coats and dresses, and the tap, tap of their red heels on the steps. How anxious they must have been, how full of emotion, how curious to peer into the future! What visions did Cagliostro evoke for them in his magic glass?…

And then I thought of Cagliostro in the dungeon of the Castle of San Leon in rags and chains, lying upon a pile of straw, the wretched victim of the Inquisition.

A door on the landing below me opened slowly and noiselessly—I stopped, scarcely breathing, in expectation of some mystic revelation. Was the phantom of the arch-necromancer coming out to greet me? No; it was but the wind! I closed the door softly behind me and hastily descended the steps.

Katterfelto

THIS LETTER APPEARED IN THE FEBRUARY 1831 ISSUE of *The Mirror of Literature, Amusement and Instruction,* a British periodical:

In reply to the question of your correspondent—"Who was Katterfelto?" I am enabled to offer the few brief paragraphs which follow. With regard to his birth, parentage and education, I am, however, not qualified to convey any information. I know not "to whom he was related, or by whom forgot." I became acquainted with him about the year 1790 or 1791, when he visited the City of Durham, accompanied by his wife and daughter. He then appeared to be about sixty years of age. His travelling equipage consisted of an old rumbling coach, a pair of sorry hacks, and two black servants. They wore green liveries with red collars, but the colours were sadly faded by long use.

Having taken suitable apartments, the black servants were sent round the town, blowing trumpets and delivering bills, announcing their master's astonishing performances, which in the day time consisted in displaying the wonders of the microscope, &c. and in the evening in exhibiting electric experiments, in the course of which he introduced his two celebrated black cats, generally denominated the Doctor's Devils—for, be it understood, that our hero went under the dignified style and title of *Doctor* Katterfelto. Tricks of legerdemain concluded the evening's entertainments.

The first night of the Doctor's performance was extremely wet, and the writer of this, who was then quite a boy, composed his whole audience. The Doctor's spouse invited me behind the curtains to the fire, on one side of which sat the great conjuror himself, his person being enveloped in an old green, greasy roquelaire, and his head decorated with a black velvet cap. On the other side of the fire-place sat Mrs. Katterfelto and daughter, in a corresponding style of dress—that is to say, equally ancient and uncleanly. The family appeared, indeed, to be in distressed circumstances....Having been admitted behind the scenes, I had an opportunity of seeing the conjuror's apparatus, but the performance was postponed to another evening.

The letter (signed "Dunelm") goes on to describe the performance that took place the following evening, before a "tolerably respectable" number of townsfolk.

Yet the question remains: "Who was Katterfelto?"

In some respects, he was a successor to Isaac Fawkes. Increasingly, Fawkes had added mechanical marvels to his show; Katterfelto demonstrated scientific wonders, and concluded with magic tricks. And if Fawkes was a pioneer of advertising, Katterfelto was a master of the art.

The son of a Prussian army officer (or so he said), Christian Wilhelm Katterfelt had a passion for scientific learning; a theatrical disposition; and a wanderlust. Accordingly, he had added an *o* to his name and become Katterfelto —scientific lecturer, itinerant showman. As such, he had roamed about in Europe for a number of years, lecturing on the latest discoveries of science (or "natural philosophy," as it was then called). Little is known of his activities during this period, though he claimed to have appeared before kings and queens. (He may or may not have.) Finally, he had boarded a ship, with his wife and six-year-old daughter, and sailed for England. Perhaps he had grown weary of the wars and turmoil on the Continent.

On September 26th, 1776, the ship docked at Hull. Katterfelto disembarked with his family, and watched as his crates were loaded onto a wagon. Ten days later he placed an ad in the *York Courant*. The first of his frequent ads in British newspapers, it introduced Katterfelto as a "Professor of Natural Philosophy, Mathematics, Astronomy, Geography, Fortification, Navigation etc." He had lectured in Hull, it noted, to "universal applause." Now he was in York, and would be exhibiting "a curious Apparatus." Listed were the location, times, and price of admission.

Katterfelto remained in York for two weeks, lecturing daily. When attendance began to slacken, he moved on to Leeds. From there he traveled to other towns in Yorkshire. In each town he would stay at an inn; engage the use of a hall; and promote himself with newspaper ads and handbills.

For several years Katterfelto toured the provinces, with his wife, daughter, and scientific apparatus. In town after town he demonstrated the wonders of science. Then, toward the end of 1780, this wandering came to a halt. A notice in the *Morning Herald* announced that Katterfelto had arrived in London.

He remained there for nearly four years. During that time he become a well-known, and controversial, figure. Initially, he had established himself in a hall known as Cox's Museum. Then he moved to a hall in Piccadilly. Its light, he explained, was better for the Solar Microscope—the apparatus that was the centerpiece of his show.

Londoners were intrigued by this showman, with his square cap, black gown, and German accent. And the lectures were well-attended, thanks to his skills as a publicist. Admissions were sold and Katterfelto prospered—so much so that he was able to purchase a coach. He also acquired two servants: a pair of African boys whom he garbed in livery. At the height of his fame, he was summoned to Windsor Castle, where he performed for the royal family.

But by 1784 his popularity in London had waned; and Katterfelto resumed his itinerant ways. For the next fifteen years he traveled the roads of England, Scotland, and Wales, rumbling along in his coach. Depending on the turnout, he would remain in a town for days, weeks, or months. (In Birmingham he stayed for nearly a year.)

To attract an audience, Katterfelto advertised—ceaselessly and shamelessly. His ads were immodest ("the greatest philosopher in this kingdom since Sir Isaac Newton"); immoderate ("the most wonderful Exhibition in the World");

and intriguing. And they were often disguised as editorial content (newspapers had no compunction about running such ads), or as testimonials. They appealed to a craving for wonders; and they promised a show that was both edifying and entertaining.

Of what did the show consist? Typically, it was divided into three parts. He began with an hour-long lecture —a discourse rendered authoritative by his accent and demeanor. Next, he conducted experiments—demonstrations of electricity, magnetism, and other phenomena. And he concluded with a magic act. Among his tricks were mindreading; a bullet catch (he caught it in a bottle); and an hourglass that stopped and started at his command. He also exposed the cheating techniques of cardsharps and others. And he introduced his black cat, whose tail was made to vanish and reappear.

This ad appeared in a London newspaper:

Great Wonders! Wonders! Wonders! Wonders! and Wonders! are now to be seen in a very warm Room, at No. 22, Piccadilly. This and every day this week, from eleven in the morning till four in the afternoon, and precisely at seven clock, every evening this week, Mr. Katterfelto will show a variety of new surprising Experiments in Natural and Experimental Philosophy and Mathematics, and his whole regular Course of Philosophical Lectures are delivered in Twelve different times, a different Lecture and Experiment every day, and every evening at 7 o'clock. His various experiments are as follow, viz.

Philosophical, Mathematical, Optical, Magnetical, Electrical, Physical, Chymical, Pneumatic, Hydraulic, Hydrostatic, Proetic, Stenographic, Blencical, Caprimantic Art.

By his new-improved Solar Microscope, will be seen many surprising insects in different waters, beer, milk, vinegar, and blood; and other curious objects.

Mr. Katterfelto has, in his travels for these eighteen years past, had the honour to exhibit with great applause before the Empress of Russia, the Queen of Hungary, the King of Prussia, Denmark, Sweden, and Polland, and before many other Princes.

And after his Lecture, Mr. Katterfelto will show and discover several New Deceptions, on Dice, Cards, Billiards, Tennis, Letters, Money, Watches, Caskets, Silver and Gold, Boxes, Medals, Pyramidical Glases, Mechanical Clocks.

Admittance, front seats 3s. second seats 2s. back seats 1s. for servants only.

The main attraction was the Solar Microscope. A combined microscope and magic lantern, it projected startling images onto a screen. Revealed were the minute organisms in a drop of liquid. This poem about the device appeared in a newspaper:

> Strange Wonders hid from human sight,
> His Microscope can bring to light,
> The works of God, unseen by eyes,
> The means of seeing, this supplies,
> All haste to him, whilst here he stayes,
> Then sing, like me, the Doctor's Praise.

The poem was probably written by Katterfelto himself.

At the conclusion of the show, items were offered for sale. One could purchase a magnet; phosphorus matches (invented by Katterfelto); a Hygrometer (a pocket-sized device that foretold changes in the weather); and—during the influenza epidemic of 1782—a nostrum called Dr. Batto's Medicine. Katterfelto bottled this concoction himself. Formulated originally, he said, by a fifteenth-century physician, it had "cured many thousand persons of the late Influenza." Earlier, with the Solar Microscope, he had shown the organisms he believed responsible for influenza.*

But the medicine was ineffectual, except as a placebo. And it contributed (along with his Tincture for the Tooth-ache and other dubious remedies) to a decline in his repu-tation. Hitherto, he had been seen as a scientific showman. But increasingly, Dr. Katterfelto (as he now styled himself) became known as a quack. In print and on the stage he was mocked. And it was as a quack that he would be remem-bered.†

During his final years as an itinerant lecturer, his for-tunes declined. Katterfelto was even arrested at one point, in Shrewsbury, and locked up as a vagrant. Yet he was able still to eke out a living. Accompanied by his wife and daughter (the two servants had been let go), he drove his coach from town to town—lecturing, conjuring, and ped-dling nostrums.

In 1799, while lecturing in the town of Bedale, he fell ill and died. Katterfelto was buried in the chancel of the local church—a mark of the respect accorded him by the townsfolk. An obituary notice—his final ad, as it were—described him as "the *wonderful* philosopher."

---

* While the particular organisms shown were not in fact respon-sible, his belief would prove to be correct: influenza was a conta-gious disease, caused by micro-organisms.

† The word *katerfelto* even entered the language, as a term for a quack or charlatan.

Robertson

THE PHANTASMAGORIA WAS ABOUT TO BEGIN. IT WAS a summer night in Paris; and an expectant audience sat in a dimly-lit hall. The hall was located inside what had been—ten years earlier, before the Revolution—the Convent of the Capucines. Packed together on benches, the Parisians were whispering to one another. They eagerly awaited a frightening show.

Earlier, they had hastened past tombs and graves; paid the price of admission; and entered the hall. They had come to the abandoned convent to experience a macabre spectacle, presented by Étienne-Gaspard Robertson. In his memoirs Robertson (1763–1837) describes the entry into the hall:

> After a number of turns that quelled any lingering impressions of the profane noise of the city; and after having traversed the cloisters of the former convent, hung with fantastical paintings; and having passed through my physics chamber, one arrived at an antique door. Covered with hieroglyphics, it seemed to announce the entrance to the mysteries of Isis. And one entered now a somber place, dimly lit by a sepulchral lamp; only some gloomy pictures announced one's destination. A profound calm, an absolute silence, a sudden isolation at the end of a noisy street—one was on the threshold of another world.*

---

* Original text: "Après plusieurs détours propres à changer l'impression que l'on conserve du bruit profane d'une grande cité, après avoir parcouru les cloîtres carrés de l'ancien couvent, décorés de peintures fantastiques, et traversé mon cabinet de physique, on arrivait devant une porte d'une forme antique, couvertes d'hiéroglyphes, et qui semblait annoncer l'entrée des mystères d'Isis. On se trouvait alors dans un lieu sombre, tendu de noir, faiblement éclairé par une lampe sépulcrale, et donc quelques images lugubres annonçaient seules la destination; un calme profond, un silence

The whispering ceased as Robertson, in formal dress, entered the hall. Thin and pale, he stood before a curtain and, with a grave countenance, addressed the audience. What transpired after death, he told them, was hidden by a veil. Men had long wondered what lay beyond that veil. Mages, sibyls, and Egyptian priests claimed to have penetrated it, with their secret arts. Tonight, he would employ those very arts in his *fantasmagorie*. Having promised to raise the dead, said Robertson, he was about to do so.

He gestured; and the lamp went out, plunging the hall into darkness. Thunder sounded. A bell began to toll. And music filled the hall—the eerie strains of a glass harmonica.*

Behind Robertson appeared a sky flashing with bolts of lightning. A point of light grew larger, and took shape as a ghostly figure. The figure advanced toward the audience, eliciting gasps and shrieks. But suddenly it was gone.

During the next hour and a half, more such figures appeared and disappeared. They frightened—and entertained—those who had paid to see them. Summoned up by Robertson were devils; dancing witches; a ghost that emerged from its grave; a winged skull that flew through the air; and, most terrifying of all, Death with his scythe—lunging at the audience! Summoned up too were the ghosts of famous men:

> Robespierre leaves his tomb, starts to stand—but lightning strikes him; and the monster and his tomb are pulverized into dust. The spirits of revered individuals—Voltaire, Lavoisier, J. J. Rousseau—appear one by one, to provide an

---

absolu, un isolement subit au sortir d'une rue bruyante, étaient comme les préludes d'une monde idéal." (from Robertson's *Mémoires récréatifs, scientifiques et anecdotiques,* 1831)

* The glass harmonica was invented by Benjamin Franklin. It consisted of a series of glass bowls, graduated in size, mounted on a rotating axle. The musician turned it by means of a foot pedal, while touching the bowls with moistened fingers. Said Chateaubriand of the glass harmonica: "The ear of a mortal can perceive in its plaintive tones the echoes of a divine harmony."

interlude of calm. And Diogenes, lantern in hand, searches for a man. He passes among the rows of seats, rudely frightening the ladies—which entertains everyone. These optical effects are such that each person thinks he can reach out and touch the figure that approaches.*

---

* "Robespierre sort de son tombeau, veut se relever......la foudre tombe et met en poudre le monstre et son tombeau. Des ombres chéries viennent adoucir le tableau: Voltaire, Lavoisier, J. J. Rousseau, paraissent tour à tour; Diogène, sa lanterne à la main, cherche un homme, et, pour le trouver, traverse pour ainsi dire les rangs, et cause impoliment aux dames une frayeur dont chacune se divertit. Tels sont les effets de l'optique, que chacun croit toucher avec la main ces objets qui s'approachent." (from a review in the *Courrier des Spectacles,* quoted in Robertson's memoirs)

Robertson concluded the show with these remarks:

> I have taken you through all the phenomena of the Phantas-
> magoria. I have revealed to you the secrets of the Egyptian
> priests and of the seers. I have tried to show you the more
> occult aspects of physics: those things that seemed super-
> natural during the centuries of credulity. But it remains for
> me to offer you something that is all too real. You who have
> perhaps smiled at my experiments; you beautiful women
> who have experienced some moments of terror—here is the
> sole spectacle that is truly terrible, truly to be feared.
> Whether you are strong, weak, or powerful, whether you
> are credulous or atheistic, good-looking or homely—behold
> the fate that awaits you! *Behold that which you will become
> one day!* And remember the Phantasmagoria.*

And a final image rose up before them: that of a human
skeleton mounted on a pedestal. Having provided them
with an evening of macabre thrills, Robertson now left his
audience with a *memento mori*—a reminder of their mortality.

Yet as they exited the hall, few were reflecting upon their
mortality. Rather, they were talking about the Phantasmagoria, and wondering how it was done. For while Robertson made clear that principles of optics were involved, he
would not divulge the details of his art.

But his secrets were finally revealed—in a lawsuit he filed
against two former assistants (who were presenting a similar
show); and years later, in his memoirs. In both of these he

---

* "J'ai parcouru tous les phénomènes de la fantasmagorie; je vous
ai dévoilé les secrets des prêtres de Memphis et des illuminés; j'ai
tâché de vous montrer ce que la physique a de plus occulte, ces
effets qui parurent surnaturels dans les siècles de la crédulité; mais
il me reste à vous en offrir un qui n'est que trop réel. Vous qui
peut-être avez souri à mes expériences, beautés qui avez éprouvé
quelques momens de terreurs, voici le seul spectacle vraiment terrible, vraiment à craindre: hommes forts, faibles, puissans, et sujets,
crédules ou athées, belles ou laides, voilà le sort qui vous est réservé,
voilà ce que vous serez un jour; souvenez-vous de la fantasmagorie."

described the device that produced the Phantasmagoria. It was a modified magic lantern, which he called the Fantascope.

Magic lanterns had been around since the 1600s (and are still with us, in the form of the slide projector). The magic lantern was an oil lamp equipped with a concave mirror and a lens. Glass slides with painted images were inserted into it; and the images were projected onto a screen. Robertson's innovation (actually, he borrowed it from another showman) was to mount the magic lantern on a trolley. By rolling it away from the screen while adjusting the lens, a startling effect was produced: the image grew in size and seemed to approach the audience. Hence the gasps and shrieks, as the scary figure came closer.

Onto what did Robertson project his images? Once the hall had been darkened, the curtain was raised. Exposed now (but unseen in the dark) was a gauze screen, which had been kept hidden from the audience. Onto it the images were projected from the rear. (Located behind the screen, the Fantascope too was unseen.) Also, images were projected onto a cloud of smoke, which Robertson generated by pouring chemicals onto a brazier. Smoke, he had found, made for a convincing ghost. Often he would use two Fantascopes at once, which allowed his phantoms to emerge from a fixed background. And he even had two-piece slides, which enabled a ghost to roll its eyes—eliciting more gasps and shrieks. Finally, his off-stage assistants provided voices for the ghosts.

In post-Revolutionary Paris, the Phantasmagoria was a popular attraction. And Étienne-Gaspard Robertson was a representative figure of his time and place. Like many intellectuals, he had succumbed to the blandishments of the Enlightenment, becoming irreligious and anti-clerical. He believed that all religions had been based on deception— that the ancient priests, of Egypt, Greece, and elsewhere, had been charlatans. They had used trickery to acquire a supernatural aura and thereby maintain their power. Indeed, said Robertson, they had used techniques and devices similar to his own.

Robertson characterized those in his audience as either *crédules* or *athées*—credulous dupes or enlightened free-thinkers. And he was staging his illusions, he told them, as s*pectacles instructifs*—edifying spectacles to counteract belief in the supernatural. Yet (as he surely knew) no one came to the Phantasmagoria to be edified. Rather, they wished to be mystified—thrilled—entertained! And Robertson, with his Fantascope, gave them what they wanted. He was a master of illusion—a conjurer whose show, usually sold-out, made him wealthy.

Though best-known as an illusionist, Robertson pursued other interests as well. He was a painter and draftsman. He gave lectures in physics, and assisted Volta in a demonstration of the effects of electricity. (Among those present at the demonstration was Napoleon.) And he was a pioneer in aeronautics. In 1803 he ascended in a balloon of his own design, setting an altitude record. And in 1806, he set a distance record for balloon flight.

In that same year the Convent of the Capucines was torn down. Founded in 1688, it had been noted for the austerity and piety of its nuns. But during the Revolution they had been driven out; and an assortment of less pious tenants had moved in. Robertson took over a hall behind the chapel, draped it in black, and staged his shows. The government established a workshop for the printing of banknotes. The painter Girodet set up a studio. Laundrywomen and other squatters settled into the abandoned rooms. And after ten o'clock at night, when Robertson's hall closed, prostitutes used its attic.

There were tenants, too, remaining from the time of the nuns. And late at night they came out. *The real ghosts* rose from the tombs and graves, gathered in the courtyard, and lamented what had befallen the convent.

Meanwhile, Robertson's ghosts—those images on slides—had been put away for the night.*

---

* Though his show was acclaimed, and brought him fame and

fortune, Robertson did not originate the Phantasmagoria. Rather, it was the creation of Paul Philidor, about whom little is known. (He seems to have been a German who had assumed a French name.) In 1793—six years before Robertson—Philidor entertained Parisians with a *fantasmagorie,* as he called it; and Robertson probably attended a performance. All the basic elements were in place: the name ("a gathering of ghosts"); spectral figures projected onto a screen; a magic lantern on wheels. His show concluded with a comic image of the Devil.

But Robertson's version was more theatrical and elaborate; and it created a sensation. As a result, imitators sprang up; and rival Phantasmagorias competed for audiences in Paris. One was that of Robertson's former assistants, who had stolen his secrets. And in 1801 a Phantasmagoria opened in London. Presenting it was Paul de Philipsthal—who is believed to have been Philidor, resurfacing with a new name after having fled France during the Terror. The show was a hit and spawned more imitators. The illusory ghosts were soon frightening American audiences, and traveling about Europe in the shows of roving Italians.

But tastes change; and by the 1840s ghost shows had become rare. Yet their influence would be lasting; for they were a forerunner of motion pictures. Moving images on a screen; music and sound effects; an enthralled audience—the ghost shows were an early form of cinema. Among the first films were those of magician Georges Méliès; and their phantoms, devils, and trick photography were clearly a legacy of the Phantasmagoria.

The shows themselves were relegated to the annals of stage magic. Then, unexpectedly, they reappeared in the twentieth century—in American movie theatres. Spook shows, as they were called, were presented at midnight (and accompanied by a horror movie). A magician would come on stage and perform. Then the lights went out, eerie music filled the theatre, and ghosts, skeletons, and zombies began to appear. These were projections on gauze screens; prop skeletons dangled on wires; and actors staggering down the aisles. And just as in the old days, shrieks were elicited.

One magician who did spook shows was Dantini the Magnificent. His story, along with that of Georges Méliès, will be told in Volume Two.

Comus

IN 1793 COMUS, A FRENCH CONJURER, TOURED THE PRO-
vincial towns of England. (Like Philidor, he may have
been a refugee from the Reign of Terror in France.) The
tour was a success; and Comus brought his show to London.
There it played for a month at No. 28, Haymarket, with
half-a-crown charged for admission.*

Comus (?–1820) was a coiner of words; and his newspaper
ad was replete with pseudo-scientific terminology. Each evening at 7:00, it announced, he would be exhibiting

> various uncommon experiments with his Enchanted Horo-
> logium, Pyxidees Literarum, and many curious operations
> in Rhabdology, Steganography, and Phylacteria, with many
> wonderful performances on the grand Dodocahedron, also
> Chartomantic Deceptions and Kharamatic Operations. To
> conclude with the performance of the Teretopæst Figure
> and Magical House; the like never seen in this kingdom
> before, and will astonish every beholder.

What were these wonders? The Enchanted Horologium
was a kind of crystal ball—a mystical device that

> by the means of an Alhadida moving on a Cathetus, dis-
> covers to the company the exact time of the day or night by
> a proposed watch, though the watch may be in any gentle-
> man's pocket, or five miles distant, if required; it also points

---

* The Comus who performed in England during the 1790s
is known to historians of magic as Comus II. There were two
Comuses—just as there would be a dozen magicians who called
themselves Signor Blitz, and even more (Hardini, Howdini,
Houdeen, Oudini, etc.) who hoped to be mistaken for Houdini.

out the colour of any lady or gentleman's clothes, by the wearer only touching it with a finger, and is further possessed of such occult qualities as to discover the thoughts of one person to another, even at an unlimited distance.

The Pyxidees Literarum was "an operation never attempted before by mankind." It would "incontestably prove that there are possible means of procuring a knowledge of future events."

Steganography was "the art of imbibing any person's thoughts in an instant, by the assistance of an invisible agent."

And the grand Dodocahedron? Surely that alone (whatever it was) had been worth the price of admission!

Torrini

IN 1858 JEAN-EUGÈNE ROBERT-HOUDIN, "THE FATHER OF modern magic," published his memoirs. In them he tells of acquiring a mentor: an itinerant magician named Torrini. Nearly sixty pages are devoted to an account of his apprenticeship with Torrini. It is a story that reads like a novel.

It begins with Torrini finding Jean alongside the road. The young man is unconscious (having flung himself from a stagecoach in a fit of fever). The magician carries Jean into his carriage—a sizeable vehicle that both serves him as a residence and converts into a theater. When Jean regains consciousness, he finds himself aboard this theater on wheels, rumbling along in the countryside.

Torrini nurses him back to health, and takes him on as an apprentice. As they travel about, Jean learns the secrets of magic; assists with the shows; and even performs. When finally he bids farewell to Torrini, he has acquired the skills for a conjuring career of his own.

It is an improbable and inspiring story. It is also (as is now believed) entirely fictional. No such person as Torrini ever existed. Rather, he is a character whom Robert-Houdin has imagined and inserted into his memoirs. The story reads like a novel because it is one.

For years, on the basis of this account, Torrini was included in histories of conjuring. He was described as an itinerant performer of the early nineteenth century—a nobleman whose real name (as revealed in the memoirs) was Edmond de Grisy. Then, in 1943, French scholar Jean Chavigny published the results of an investigation. He had searched for evidence of Torrini's (or de Grisy's) historicity, and could find none. No trace of this person could be found, other than his depiction in the memoirs of Robert-Houdin. Chavigny's conclusion? Torrini was a literary device—a character whom Robert-Houdin had invented, to enliven the recounting of his early years.

Other scholars have concurred in declaring Torrini to be fictional, as has Robert-Houdin's grandson. And they have speculated as to the motivation for this literary malfeasance. According to one theory, Torrini represents a surrogate father—one who (unlike his actual father) encourages Jean to pursue a career as a conjurer. Another has it that Torrini—a nobleman who has become a magician—is meant to elevate the social status of the profession. And yet another suggests that the Torrini tale allows Robert-Houdin to withhold the real story of his beginnings as a conjurer.

Or perhaps deception—for the purpose of entertaining—is simply standard practice for a conjurer.

In any case, a fictional magician would ordinarily have been excluded from these pages. But Torrini has earned himself a place—with a memorable trick that he performed at the Vatican.

Torrini had been invited, says Robert-Houdin, to perform for the Pope. He knew that a certain cardinal would be in attendance, who owned a rare and costly watch. Unusually large, this watch was supposedly the only one of its kind. Torrini managed, however, to obtain a duplicate. He had a watchmaker engrave it with the cardinal's insignia. Thus, the two watches were indistinguishable.

The performance went well, with the Pope and his court mystified and amused by the tricks. To conclude the show, Torrini asked if he might borrow a watch—the largest one available. The Pope ordered the cardinal to lend his watch. Reluctantly, the cardinal handed it to Torrini.

Whereupon, Torrini flung it to the ground and stamped on it repeatedly—smashing it to pieces, as the cardinal watched in horror.

Presenting him with the remains, Torrini asked the cardinal to confirm that this was indeed his watch. The cardinal murmured that it was. The Pope too inspected the remains of the watch. As he did so, Torrini slipped the duplicate

watch into his pocket.

Torrini announced that he would use his powers to restore the watch to its original state. "And the restoration shall take place," he said, "as the watch passes into the pocket of a person who cannot be suspected of complicity."

"Aha!" said the Pope, laughing. "Wouldn't that be something! But what would you do, my good sorcerer, if I asked you to choose *my* pocket?"

"Your Holiness need only give the order and I shall obey."

"Let it be so."

By sleight of hand Torrini caused the shattered watch to vanish. And the Pope, reaching into his pocket, cried out in astonishment. For there was the watch, intact!

Word of the feat spread, creating a sensation in Rome. And audiences flocked to see Torrini perform, says Robert-Houdin. The publicity had been worth the cost of the duplicate watch.

Torrini is a unique figure in the annals of magic. Robert-Houdin—the father of modern magic—claimed him as a mentor and described his career in detail. Yet he never existed.

An illusionist who was an illusion himself!*

---

* A real-life magician, Howard Thurston, performed a similar trick in 1924 for President Coolidge. Invited to entertain at the White House, Thurston learned that Coolidge had been presented with a special watch by the Massachusetts legislature. He was able to procure a duplicate.

The performance took place in the East Room, where a stage had been set up. Thurston borrowed the watch from Coolidge, placed it on a table, and raised a hammer over it. In *My Life of Magic* (1929), he describes what ensued:

"The hammer descended with a whang. The casing of the watch fell apart, the works flew in all directions. Somebody uttered an audible cry of alarm and I could sense that others were holding their breath, so tense had the silence become. I shot a glance at the President. He had not moved a muscle; his chin rested in his hand; his keen blue eyes looked into mine, as much as to say, 'I don't believe it!' He was the calmest person in the room."

Thurston gathered up the broken pieces, wrapped them in a paper, and made them disappear. On the table was a loaf of bread that had been brought from the kitchen. Handing a knife to Mrs. Coolidge, Thurston asked her to cut open the loaf. And inside was found the President's watch, intact. Thurston returned it to him.

"My visit to the White House had given me a chance to see the leader of our nation at close range. His human qualities, his calm wholesomeness and his imperturbability left me with a strong impression of the breadth of his character."

Signor Blitz

IN 1810, THE YEAR OF SIGNOR BLITZ'S BIRTH, SUPERSTI-
tion was supposedly in retreat. Popular beliefs about
magical powers, witchcraft, divination, the Devil, etc.
were giving way, it was assumed, to reason—to rational ways
of thinking—to the intellectual advances of the Enlightenment. Yet when Blitz began his career as a conjurer, he
found, to his surprise, that such beliefs still were flourishing.

Antonio van Zandt (his given name) was born in Deal,
a seaside town in England. He learned his first tricks from
Gypsies who frequented the town. At the age of thirteen he
made his debut on a stage. And within a few years he was
earning a living and gaining a reputation, as Signor Blitz.
Audiences applauded his deceptions and his showmanship.

At the same time, however, he was being denounced.
There were clergymen who viewed him as a pernicious
influence—a practitioner of the black arts, in league with
the Devil. And there were towns in which he was forbidden
to perform, or was even arrested and brought before a magistrate. To his amazement, Blitz was credited with actual
powers and accused of practicing sorcery—in nineteenth-
century Britain!

In his memoirs, *Fifty Years in the Magic Circle* (1871), Signor
Blitz recalls these accusations. In Glasgow, for example, his
shows drew a mixed reaction:

> Of the thousands who came to see me, hundreds returned
> home with the full conviction that I was either the d__l
> [devil] himself or closely allied to his satanic majesty. The
> whole population became greatly excited, some appearing
> friendly, while others, incompetent to distinguish between
> the supernatural and the real, characterized me as deserv-
> ing the fate of the witches and wizards of old, whose temer-
> ity was rewarded on the scaffold.

And in Manchester, he was visited one morning by a clergyman. "Signor Blitz," said his visitor, "I am a minister of the Gospel in this city, and I have solicited this interview to remonstrate with you upon the impropriety and error of your ways. You are leading thousands of poor sinners to Satan."

He accused Blitz of being a necromancer, at war with religion and morality. When Blitz asked how else he was to make a living, being unacquainted with any other pursuit, the clergyman rose slowly; pointed to the tables full of magical apparatus; and said, in an animated tone: "Throw away that trumpery, Signor Blitz, and turn from wickedness to righteousness, for blessed are the good!"

Blitz sought to defend himself. There was nothing sinful in his art, he protested. He was no evil spirit in form or in principle. Rather, his shows demonstrated that mechanical inventions, and dexterity of hand, were more wonderful than the mysteries of ancient magicians. He offered, nonetheless, to listen to any advice the clergyman might have to offer.

"Preach the Gospel, Signor Blitz, and live for heaven."

Blitz saw that it was pointless to continue. And he decided to punish the clergyman for his unwarranted air of assurance. Employing that dexterity of hand, he slipped a snuff-box into the clergyman's pocket. Then he announced that the interview would have to conclude, as he had another appointment.

The clergyman headed for the door. But as he reached it, Blitz demanded that he return the snuff-box. "I do not understand you, sir," said the clergyman, puzzled. "I have no box."

"I understand *you* perfectly well, sir. You came here under the plea of preaching the Gospel, and stole my snuff-box."

Indignant, the clergyman denied the charge. But threatened with a search of his coat, he reached into his pocket, discovered the snuff-box, and turned pale. "It is incomprehensible!" he cried. And handing over the box, he bounded down the stairs and fled the premises.

Blitz was bewildered by the antagonism of such people. But equally bewildering were those who credited him with supernatural powers and begged him to use those powers in their behalf. "There was no escape for me," he laments, "either from the importunities of the illiterate or the demands of the wise and learned, for *all* looked upon me as capable of exercising my art either for good or evil."

And he tells of a man in Mobile, Alabama, who sought his help in tracking down a thief:

> One morning I was waited upon by a venerable-looking gentleman, with gray hair. He proclaimed his unlimited confidence in my knowledge of astrology and those sciences by which light and darkness are penetrated, and the evil-doers discovered. He had been the victim of some thief: his watch, diamond ring, and several hundred dollars had been taken from him, and he had failed to discover the perpetrators.

Signor Blitz insisted that he possessed no such knowledge, and was unable to discover evil-doers. Nonetheless, Blitz accompanied the man to his residence and was introduced to his family—as a magician who was going to solve the theft. And Blitz knew at once who the thief was; for the man's son had suddenly become nervous. Blitz looked the son in the eye, but said nothing. And promising to give the matter some thought, he returned to the hall where he was performing.

Soon thereafter, the son entered the hall and confessed to the crime. He had become an habitué of the gaming-table, he told Blitz, and had stolen his father's valuables to pay his debts. Just last night, however, his luck had changed. He had won a large sum of money and been able to recover the watch and ring. And he had come now to plead with the magician. He begged Blitz not to expose him, and to somehow restore the valuables to his father, without revealing who had taken them.

I entertained a sympathy for his position, and felt it a duty to relieve his embarrassment, and probably enjoy the proud satisfaction of preserving him from destruction. I addressed him on the evil path he was pursuing, the ruin and disgrace that must eventually follow. I desired him, by all those principles which endear us to manhood, and the sacred ties that bound him to his family, to avoid the sin and destruction of a gambler's life; that I would convey the valuables to his father by means that would appear equally inexplicable as was their removal.

The son pledged never again to gamble; gave Blitz the money and stolen articles; and thanking him profusely, departed.

The magician pondered for a moment. Then he wrote a note to the father. It requested his attendance at the show that evening, and indicated that the recovery of his valuables was imminent.

That evening the father, along with his son and daughter, was in the audience. The curtain rose and the show began. Midway through it, Blitz came down into the audience. He borrowed the father's hat and showed it to be empty. Then he drew from it the watch, ring, and money, and presented them to their owner.

"The thanks I received from the gentleman were many," he reports, "and his entreaties for an explanation not less urgent."

Blitz also tells of being sought out as a fortuneteller. And in Havana, he was believed to be a *brujo*—a sorcerer with the powers to heal:

I was considered by some as the author of all misfortunes; yet the deaf, blind, crippled, and the afflicted of every kind, sanguine of my powers to benefit their condition, visited me constantly; from morning until night they crowded my residence, importuning me to prescribe remedies for their recovery—to exercise such potent spells as were at my command. Their entreaties were unceasing and earnest,

and all efforts on my part to disabuse and enlighten their thoughts in respect to my vocation, its duties, and my powerless position over spiritual events, were unavailing. I told them that the Great Master of heaven and earth directed and distributed His favors agreeable to His wisdom; that it was to Him they must appeal.

The career of Signor Blitz spanned half a century. Initially, he mystified audiences in England, Scotland, and Ireland. But in 1834 he sailed to America and performed in its principal cities. Blitz liked the openness and friendliness of Americans. He appreciated too that he was not denounced as a devil. And he wound up staying for the rest of his life, making his home in Philadelphia.

His show was both mystifying and amusing. A variety act, it consisted of magic tricks, ventriloquism (he was one of the first ventriloquists to use a dummy), trained canaries, juggling, and plate-spinning. ("The evening's entertainment," promised his ad, "will conclude with the celebrated Dance of Six Dinner Plates on a common table.")

Blitz was popular with audiences throughout the country —so much so that he spawned a host of imitators:

> In later years this has proved an incalculable annoyance, there being not less than thirteen people travelling the country using my name and profession, circulating a verbatim copy of my handbill and advertisement—not only assuming to be the *original* Blitz, but in many instances claiming to be a son or nephew. I have been in constant receipt of bills of their contracting, for, not content with taking my name, they have not even honor enough to pay their debts. The thirteen now travelling in the United States exhibit under the following, and other names:
>
> > Signor Blitz.
> > Signor Blitz, Jr.
> > Signor Blitz, The Original.
> > Signor Blitz's Son.
> > Signor Blitz's Nephew.
> > Signor Blitz, The Great.
> > Signor Blitz, The Wonderful.
> > Signor Blitz, The Unrivalled.
> > Signor Blitz, The Mysterious.
> > Signor Blitz, By Purchase.
> > Signor Blitz, The Great Original.

Despite the competition, the actual Signor Blitz remained in demand and became wealthy. During his later years he performed solely for charitable institutions. And during the Civil War, he entertained wounded soldiers at hospitals, giving more than a hundred performances.

Blitz died in 1877, at his home in Philadelphia; he was survived by a wife and four children. An obituary in *The New York Times* observed: "He was a great favorite, being very affable in his manners, and it will be a long while before the pleasant memories of Signor Blitz, and his wonderful boy 'Bobby' [his dummy], are effaced from the minds of the residents of Philadelphia."*

---

* Twelve years later the *Times* once again published an obituary for Signor Blitz, identifying him as the "prestidigitateur who was famous a quarter of a century ago." This latter deceased was apparently one of the impostors!

Maelzel

IN DECEMBER OF 1835, JOHANN MAELZEL EXHIBITED HIS chess-playing automaton in Richmond, Virginia. Among those who attended was Edgar Allan Poe, editor of the *Southern Literary Messenger*. A few months later, Poe published an essay titled "Maelzel's Chess-Player." It begins:

> Perhaps no exhibition of the kind has ever elicited so general attention as the Chess-Player of Maelzel. Wherever seen it has been an object of intense curiosity to all persons who think. Yet the question of its *modus operandi* is still undetermined. Nothing has been written on this topic which can be considered as decisive—and accordingly we find everywhere men of mechanical genius, of great general acuteness and discriminative understanding, who make no scruple in pronouncing the Automaton *a pure machine,* unconnected with human agency in its movements, and consequently, beyond all comparison, the most astonishing of the inventions of mankind. And such it would undoubtedly be, were they right in their supposition.

But Poe rejects that supposition. He compares the Chess-Player with other automata (including a mechanical duck that produced "the sound of quacking in the most natural manner"), and with the calculating machine of Thomas Babbage. And he concludes that it cannot possibly be a pure machine—that someone must be operating it. "The only question then is of the *manner* in which human agency is brought to bear."

The Chess-Player was invented, Poe tells us, in 1769 by a Hungarian nobleman named Kempelen. For many years Kempelen exhibited it throughout Europe. Finally, it was sold to Maelzel, who conducted his own series of tours. Maelzel was currently visiting the principal cities of the

53

U.S.; and Richmond (where he had exhibited the automaton once before) was his latest stop.

Poe describes the Chess-Player. Maelzel had rolled into view a cabinet on wheels. On top of it was a chessboard. Attached to the rear was a chair, in which was seated a life-like representation of a Turk. Legs crossed, the turbaned figure—a mannequin in Oriental garb—was holding a long pipe in one hand; its other hand lay beside the chessboard.

To allay suspicions of a human operator, Maelzel displayed the interior of the Chess-Player. The cabinet was divided into two compartments—each with front and rear doors—and a drawer. Maelzel opened the doors and illuminated the interior with a candle. The cabinet was shown to be empty, except for an array of machinery—gears, wheels, levers—in one compartment, and similar components in the other.

> The whole box being thus apparently disclosed to the scrutiny of the company, Maelzel, still leaving the doors and drawer open, rolls the Automaton entirely round, and exposes the back of the Turk by lifting up the drapery. A door about ten inches square is thrown open in the loins of the figure, and a smaller one also in the left thigh. The interior of the figure, as seen through these apertures, appears to be crowded with machinery. In general, every spectator [with the exception of Poe, as we shall see] is now thoroughly satisfied of having beheld and completely scrutinized, at one and the same time, every individual portion of the Automaton, and the idea of any person being concealed in the interior, during so complete an exhibition of that interior, if ever entertained, is immediately dismissed as preposterous in the extreme.

Maelzel then closed the doors. Inserting a large key, he wound up the automaton. And a chess game ensued, with the spectators (Poe in particular) paying close attention. The contest was between the Turk and a challenger from the audience. A whir of machinery was heard, as the Turk

lifted its arm, grasped its pieces, and moved them. Maelzel moved the pieces for the challenger.

> During the progress of the game, the figure now and then rolls its eyes, as if surveying the board, moves its head, and pronounces the word *echec* (check) when necessary....Upon beating the game, he waves his head with an air of triumph, looks round complacently upon the spectators, and drawing his left arm farther back than usual, suffers his fingers alone to rest upon the cushion. In general, the Turk is victorious—once or twice he has been beaten. The game being ended, Maelzel will again, if desired, exhibit the mechanism of the box, in the same manner as before. The machine is then rolled back, and a curtain hides it from the view of the company.

Poe reviews the theories that have been put forth regarding the Chess-Player. He scornfully rejects the view that it is a true automaton. Some theories he deems to be untenable (for example, that Maelzel uses magnets to guide the Turk's arm); some are absurd (a small boy is hidden in the drawer); while others are plausible. In any case, he is convinced that "human agency" is involved. All that machinery inside? He is not fooled by it. Nor is he fooled by an aberration: the Turk's hand occasionally fails to grasp a chessman; nonetheless, it continues on to the intended square, as if in possession of the piece. Poe sees through this ruse. It is intended, he says, to mislead the audience—to give the impression that the Turk is entirely mechanical.

So what controls the movements of the arm? What is the *modus operandi* of the Chess-Player? There is only one possible answer, insists Poe. *A person is concealed inside.* Someone is operating the Chess-Player from within.

Yet the cabinet was shown to be empty, except for machinery. To alleviate suspicion, the doors were opened and the interior displayed. If an operator was in there, why was he not exposed?

He was not exposed, says Poe, because never were all of the doors open at once—a fact artfully obscured by Maelzel. (To confirm this, Poe made repeat visits to the exhibition.) There had always been some portion of the interior that the audience could not scrutinize.

Thus, by shifting his position as the doors were opened and closed—by contorting himself into unexposed spaces—by squeezing in behind the machinery and extending his legs behind the open drawer—the operator had remained hidden from view. Inside the cabinet was a chess-player, who was also a contortionist.

Having insisted that someone is concealed inside, Poe then goes even further—he identifies that person!

> There is a man, *Schlumberger,* who attends him [Maelzel] wherever he goes, but who has no ostensible occupation other than that of assisting in the packing and unpacking of the Automaton. This man is about the medium size, and has a remarkable stoop in the shoulders. Whether he

professes to play chess or not, we are not informed. It is quite certain, however, that he is never to be seen during the exhibition of the Chess-Player, although frequently visible just before and just after the exhibition. Moreover, some years ago Maelzel visited Richmond with his automata, and exhibited them, we believe, in the house now occupied by M. Bossieux as a dancing academy. *Schlumberger* was suddenly taken ill, and during his illness there was no exhibition of the Chess-Player.... The inferences from all this we leave, without farther comment, to the reader.

The essay concludes on a note of triumph. "We do not believe," says Poe, "that any reasonable objections can be urged against this solution of the Automaton Chess-Player."

●

Was Poe's solution correct? By and large, it was. Confirmation is provided by Signor Blitz, who once performed on the same program as Maelzel. In his memoirs Blitz reveals the following:

> The Chess Player was ingeniously constructed—a perfect counterpart of a magician's trick-table with a variety of partitions and doors, which, while they removed every possible appearance of deception, only produced greater mystery, and provided more security to the invisible player. The drawers and closets were so arranged as to enable him to change his position according to circumstances: at one moment he would be in this compartment; the next, in that; then in the body of the Turk, which permitted Maelzel to open all parts at one time.... There was a considerable display of superbly-finished machinery in the box... the object of this being to distract attention, and impress the mind with the conviction that the mystery was in the mechanism.

And Blitz names the invisible player. It was indeed Schlumberger.*

Poe was not the first to guess, and to offer an account of, the secret workings of the automaton. Several exposés had already been published—in particular, that of Sir David Brewster (which Poe refers to and incorporates into his account). But Poe's approach to the problem was uniquely his own. He brought to it his powers of observation and analysis. He proceeded methodically, like a detective. And he presented his solution in a masterful essay—an essay that prefigures the detective tale.

Poe has been acknowledged as the inventor of the detective tale. His fictional detective, C. Auguste Dupin, is featured in three tales, beginning with "The Murders in the Rue Morgue." Dupin is a master of analysis, or "ratiocination," as Poe calls it. In that first tale, published in 1841, Poe offers this description of the analytic faculty:

The mental features discoursed of as the analytical...are always to their possessor, when inordinately possessed, a source of the liveliest enjoyment. As the strong man exults in his physical ability, delighting in such exercises as call his muscles into action, so glories the analyst in that moral activity which *disentangles.* He derives pleasure from even the most trivial occupations bringing his talent into play. He is fond of enigmas, of conundrums, of hieroglyphics; exhibiting in his solutions of each a degree of *acumen* which appears to the ordinary apprehension præternatural. His

---

* Guillaume Schlumberger was a young chess-player whom Maelzel had recruited at a cafe in Paris. According to George Allen's "The History of the Automaton Chess-Player in America" (1859), Schlumberger was "not the 'Director' of the Automaton alone, but also Maelzel's 'Assistant' in his exhibitions. He acted, moreover, as a kind of confidential secretary and clerk; at one time writing his letters, at another time going round to different mechanics, who were kept busy.... Maelzel appears not only to have valued his services very highly, but also to have delighted in his society, and to have become attached to him personally."

results, brought about by the very soul and essence of method, have, in truth, the whole air of intuition.

Dupin is portrayed as the embodiment of that talent. But six years earlier, a similar talent was displayed by Poe himself. Applying the same skills that would distinguish his fictional sleuth, he penetrated the mystery of the Chess-Player.

•

For many years Maelzel exhibited the Chess-Player in the capitals of Europe. Then, during the final decade of his life, he toured with it in the U.S. (to which he had fled to escape debts and lawsuits). Rarely, though, did he exhibit only the Chess-Player. Shown with it were various mechanical devices—true automata of his own making. For Johann Maelzel was a gifted inventor as well as showman.

He was born in Regensburg, the son of an organ-builder. As a youth he was trained in music. He went on to study mathematics and mechanics, and to experiment with mechanical devices. Taking up residence in Vienna, he constructed musical automata. And he began to travel about, exhibiting them. Eventually, his abilities won him an appointment as Imperial Court Mechanician.

Among his inventions were the Panharmonicon, which duplicated the sounds of an entire orchestra (and for which Beethoven wrote *Wellington's Victory*); the Automaton Trumpeter—a soldier that played martial music (as Maelzel accompanied him on the piano); and mechanical songbirds. But his most spectacular creation was the *Conflagration of Moscow*—a diorama that consisted of a model of the city, hundreds of tiny mechanical figures, and elaborate special effects. Yet these inventions have been forgotten; and Maelzel is remembered today only as the exhibitor of Kempelen's Chess-Player.

What kind of man was Maelzel? According to Signor Blitz, he was "a large, phlegmatic man, extremely irritable, yet very kind, and he displayed great taste and refinement in all his arrangements, without regard to cost....a man of splendid attainments as a mechanic and musician, a fine linguist, and superior mathematician."

His career was a long one; and it brought him fame and financial reward (often squandered in extravagant spending). But in 1838 it came to a sad end. Signor Blitz tells the story:

> In the winter following I met Maelzel in Havana, Cuba. He had visited the city previously, and was highly successful; but this, his second venture, terminated most unfortunately, for his business failed, his exhibitions were less attended, while his pecuniary matters became desperate and gloomy. While thus discouraged and surrounded by difficulties, Schlomberg died of a fever. Maelzel was now an old man, reduced in circumstances and involved in debt, obstacles unknown to him before; his pride and spirit could not battle with the change. He secured a passage for Philadelphia, but grief produced a severe illness, which terminated in death during the voyage. Poor man! he was buried in the sea, and his effects sold at auction, to liquidate the cost of passage and other claims. The chess-player was purchased by several liberal gentlemen as a memento of the renown it had acquired in Europe and this country, and was occasionally used by amateur players in its original capacity, until it was destroyed by fire at the Chinese Museum.*

An obituary praised Maelzel, whose "ingenuity seemed to breathe life into the works of his hands." Missed would be the "kindly smile that he had for children" and "the furrow of thought that marked his brow as he inspected the movements of the famous Turk." He had moved on, it was

---

* One of the purchasers was Dr. John Kearsley Mitchell, a physician in Philadelphia. Dr. Mitchell had been acquainted with Maelzel, whose home was in Philadelphia. Oddly enough, Poe was living in the city at the time; and Dr. Mitchell was his physician.

hoped, to "where the music of his Harmonicons will be exceeded; but his body will rest beneath the blue waves of the Atlantic, till the 'last Trumpet' shall sound for the convocation of the quick and the dead."

As for the Turk, it wound up in a museum. Henry Ridgely Evans describes its final days:

> In the old Chinese Museum of Philadelphia (formerly Peales), so called because of a collection of Chinese curios displayed in its long hall, there stood in the year 1840, in a small apartment in the rear little frequented by visitors, an automaton figure, forlorn-looking and covered with dust. Thousands of persons passed through the museum during the fourteen years android occupied its inconspicuous corner, but no one inquired about and few ever laid eyes on it; it was to all intents and purposes dead to the world.

The automaton had ceased to play chess. And in 1854 it was destroyed in a fire.*

●

By what means was the Turk able to play chess? As Poe and others surmised, there was an operator inside the cabinet; and by shifting his position, he remained unseen as the interior was exposed to view. According to Poe, he then climbed into the body of the Turk, from which he was able to view the chessboard; follow his opponent's moves; and guide the arm of the Turk. But in this part of his solution, Poe was wrong. In fact, the operator remained inside the cabinet. With him in there was a second chessboard (along

---

* The Turk did not have to wait for that "last Trumpet" to sound, in order to be resurrected. John Gaughan, a builder of stage illusions, re-created the Chess-Player in his workshop. And in 1989, at a Los Angeles conference on the history of magic, his Chess-Player was pitted against a computer. Gaughan displayed its interior, to show that no one was inside; but the audience was skeptical.

with a candle). On this board he duplicated the moves being made by his opponent on the board overhead—moves revealed to him by an ingenious system of magnets.

And how was the Turk able to pick up and move its pieces? This was the most ingenious feature of all. Controlling its arm was a set of levers called a pantograph. As the operator made his moves on the inside board, the pantograph guided the arm—reproducing the moves on the outside board.

These details were revealed in an article by Dr. Silas Weir Mitchell. The son of its final owner, Mitchell had grown up with the Chess-Player and was familiar with its secret workings.

Robert Heller

I N *THE OLD AND THE NEW MAGIC* (1909), HENRY RIDGELY Evans tells of seating himself on a historic piece of furniture:

> I went on one occasion to dine with Mr. Francis J. Martinka, and while waiting for the repast to be served, seated myself upon an old-fashioned sofa in his drawing-room.
>
> "Pardon me," said my host, gaily, "while I put a bottle of wine on ice. I will be back in a little while. In the meantime, you may amuse yourself looking over those photos of eminent conjurers. And, by the way, you are seated on the very sofa which Robert Heller used in his second-sight trick. Examine it carefully and you will see where the wires and electric battery were located. I came into possession of the relic after the death of Heller."
>
> So saying he went out to look after the wine.*

The sofa was the one on which Heller's assistant had sat, while receiving "clairvoyant" impressions. Evans describes the memories that it prompted:

> In imagination that old sofa carried me back thirty years into the past. I was seated in the gallery of the old National

---

* Martinka was the proprietor of a magic shop on Sixth Avenue in New York. Located there since the mid 1870s, the shop had become a meeting place for magicians. Among those who hung out in its backroom were Heller, Herrmann the Great, and Houdini. But amateurs too were often welcome; and Henry Ridgely Evans had joined the backroom gatherings.

Francis Martinka and his brother had emigrated from Essen, Germany, where they had been engaged in a similar business. Skilled craftsman, they manufactured much of the paraphernalia sold in their shop.

Theatre, Washington, D.C., at a *soirée magique* of the famous Heller. I shall never forget his second-sight trick. It was the most wonder-provoking, the most mysterious experiment I have ever seen. In his hands, it was perfect.

Evans relates what little was known at the time of Heller's life. And he includes a photo of the magician (whose mustache was a Victorian extravaganza). But more has since become known about Robert Heller; and there has been a growing appreciation of his importance. "He gave magic and magicians a standing in America, which previously neither had had," writes John Mulholland, another historian of magic. "Earlier performers had not his finesse, his cultured manner, nor his delightfully unpretentious delivery."

William Henry Palmer (his original name) was born in 1829 in Faversham, England. He was the son of a church organist. At fourteen he entered the Royal Academy of Music on a scholarship. And he would probably have become a musician like his father, had he not—at the age of nineteen—attended a magic show. The magician was Robert-Houdin, who had brought his *Soirées Fantastiques* to a London theatre. Inspired by the show, Palmer began to study the art of conjuring with the proprietor of a magic shop.

After several years he was ready to perform. He adopted a stage name (one that resembled "Robert-Houdin"); leased the Strand Theatre; and presented a show of his own, titled *Soirées Mystérieuses of Robert Heller*. Many of the tricks he had copied from those of Robert-Houdin. Heller even mimicked the magician himself, wearing a dark curly wig and speaking with a French accent.

The show was only a modest success. And after a brief tour with it, Heller glimpsed greater opportunities in America. So in August 1852, he boarded a ship and set sail for New York. He was traveling with trunkfuls of props.

In New York he rented a theatre called Buckley's Minstrel Hall, and renamed it Heller's Saloon of Wonders. And still impersonating a Frenchman, he presented his show. "ROBERT HELLER gives an entertainment this week at his Saloon, No. 539 Broadway," reported the *Times.* "He is said [no doubt by Heller himself] to be the *Prince of Wizards.*" The show received good reviews and played for six months. Heller then traveled to Philadelphia, for a month-long stay. It was in Philadelphia that he finally dropped the French accent, and developed his own persona as a magician.

The shows were well-attended and earned him a considerable amount of money. Unfortunately, Heller lost it all in a swindle. The circumstances are murky. But he wrote to a friend that he had been "shamelessly robbed...by the Yankees." He was thinking of returning to England, he said. Meanwhile, the young magician found himself penniless, in debt, and stranded in Washington.

So, putting aside magic, he fell back on his musical training. Heller found work in Washington as a church organist. (He was using now his given name of Palmer, perhaps to avoid creditors.) He also gave piano lessons to the children of wealthy residents of the city. These lessons led to his remaining in America. For he married one of his pupils, the daughter of a banker.

But he had not given up on magic. He continued to hone his skills. And in 1861 he returned to New York and relaunched his show. The venue was the French Theatre— or Heller's Salle Diabolique, as he renamed it. A newspaper ad declared: "As Houdin is in Paris, so Heller is in New York."

Years later, *The Sphinx* (a journal for magicians) would recall:

> Heller's revised program was an immediate success. His own personality was most winning, his magic and mind-reading were superb, and his music running from classical to humorous added a delightful interlude. His patter was truly witty and his stage presence compelling.

The magic must indeed have been superb; for the shows were frequently sold-out. Heller gave nearly 400 performances at the Salle Diabolique. During the years of the Civil War, his show remained a popular attraction in New York.

After the war he performed in theatres throughout the U.S. Then, in 1869, he embarked upon a world tour. By the time the tour ended—it lasted six years—Robert Heller had become as widely known as Robert-Houdin.

His show was advertised as an evening of "Magic, Music, and Mirth." It was a unique blend of the three. The magic, which included a disappearing piano, was skillfully executed. But what made it memorable was the style with which it was presented—the *personality* of the magician. As for music, it was provided by Heller himself. He would sit down at the piano (which had yet to disappear) and give a short recital. One of his assistants described him as "a brilliant pianist ranking with some of the best of his time." Finally, the mirth added a light note to the black arts of a conjurer.

But the main attraction of the evening—the trick that everyone was waiting for—was the Second Sight Mystery.

The Second Sight Mystery was an act that mystified audiences for years. After his death, the *Times* would recall how "the amusement-loving citizens of New-York were mystified beyond measure by the second sight performances of Robert Heller. They were the talk of the town for many days, because they seemed to be outside the pale of ordinary feats of legerdemain and to have an almost supernatural character."

The act began with Heller being joined on the stage by his assistant, whom he introduced as his sister, Miss Haidee Heller. Haidee was clairvoyant, said Heller. He seated her on a sofa, with her back to the audience, and blindfolded her securely. Then he circulated among the audience, asking to be handed any article—a hat, a coin, a pocket watch. Holding up each article, he asked Haidee to name it. And astonishingly, she was able to do so.

How was it done? The "clairvoyance" was in fact a feat of memory—one that involved an elaborate code. Heller had compiled a long list of common articles, and grouped them

into sets of ten. There were nineteen of these sets. Each was linked to a particular question, such as "What is this?" "What am I holding?" "Have you got it?" The items within a set were numbered from 1 to 10; and these numbers too were linked to questions.

Both Heller and Haidee had committed the code to memory. Thus, by asking an "innocent" question, Heller was able to indicate the set that included the article. Then, with a second question, he communicated its number within the set. Haidee now knew the identity of the article. She pretended, however, to be struggling to receive a mental impression. When at last she named it, the audience broke into applause—and was utterly mystified.

But Heller knew that his words were being scrutinized, by those in the audience who suspected a code. So midway through the act—to confound such persons—he would switch to a different method. Henry Ridgely Evans describes it:

Evoking the aid of electricity, Robert Heller was enabled to convey the cue words and numbers of the sets to Miss Heller *without speaking a word*. It was this wonderful effect which so puzzled everybody. A confederate sat among the spectators, near the center aisle of the theatre, and the wires of an electric battery were connected with his chair, the electric push button being under the front part of his seat. Heller gave the cue to the set in which the article was, its number, etc., by some natural movement of his body or arms; and the confederate, rapidly interpreting the secret signals, telegraphed them to the clairvoyant on the stage. The receiving instrument was attached to the sofa upon which Miss Heller sat. The interchangeable use of the two methods of conveying information—spoken and unspoken —during an evening, completely bewildered the spectators.

None of this was revealed during his lifetime; and audiences continued to be mystified. When pressed by an interviewer to reveal how the trick was done, Heller would only say: "It is, as I have before explained—as near as I may explain it without telling you its secret—a mental operation produced by two persons whose minds are in perfect harmony with each other."*

Upon returning from his world tour, Heller reestablished himself in New York. He performed regularly at the Globe, or Heller's Wonder Theatre, as it was now called. He also had engagements in other cities. Neither his energy on stage nor his showmanship had flagged. "The great secret of my success," he once wrote to a friend, "is the *go go go* for 2 hours—no break—no time lost—every minute occupied."

But it was all about to end.

---

* The interviewer, who had dined with them, noted of Haidee: "At the dinner-table her conversational powers shone to great advantage. Familiar with the topics of the times, her remarks were as entertaining and brilliant as her manner was fascinating." The magician and his assistant were evidently two of a kind—kindred spirits—and thus able to harmonize.

On November 26, 1878, Heller opened in Philadelphia. It was a Monday evening. For a week he had been suffering from a cold; and it had grown worse. Midway through the show, he became ill. But he managed to complete the show; and he and Haidee returned to their hotel.

Not until morning was a doctor summoned. By then Heller's condition (it was probably pneumonia) had become critical. Nothing could be done. And just after midnight, he died.

Robert Heller was worth a great deal when he died. In his will he made bequests to members of his family—and to Haidee, who was not actually his sister. He also included this instruction:

> I hereby direct my Executrix…under the direction and supervision of Haidee Heller, to destroy, break up, and beat out of shape all the secret apparatus, arrangements, and mechanical devices appertaining to or in any way affecting or connected with my business, so that no one may have the benefit of my brains after my death.

Why would he have ordered this? To an outsider, the directive seems churlish and uncharitable. But magicians have always been a secretive fraternity—and a larcenous one. They have routinely copied, borrowed, and stolen from one another. (Heller himself copied from Robert-Houdin.) Apparently, the thought of rival magicians acquiring his equipment, learning his secrets, and passing his tricks off as their own, was more than Heller could bear. (At least two other magicians, Houdini and Johann Hofzinser, have left similar instructions.) In any case, he ordered that everything be destroyed.

But the destruction was never carried out. Haidee reported that, on his death-bed, Heller had revoked the order. Give it all to Hartz the magic dealer, he had instructed her, to be put up for sale.

●

Thus did that sofa—the one on which Haidee had sat and received "mental impressions"—wind up in Martinka's drawing-room. He eventually sold it to a young mentalist named Joseph Dunninger. Its current whereabouts (if it still exists) are unknown.

And what became of Haidee? For a while she remained in New York. The *Mirror* reported that she was planning to write a history of Heller's life and adventures. It is not known how far she got on such a book. Yet no one was in a better position to write it. Haidee had worked closely with Heller for nearly a decade. Moreover, they had almost certainly been lovers.*

The following year Haidee returned to England. For while not related to Heller, she was in fact English. Apparently, he had met her while performing in London in 1868, and hired her as an assistant. Initially, she had appeared in a trick called the Marvelous Hatful. Heller would borrow a hat, take it on stage, and pull from it a folded dress. The dress had grown bulkier and bulkier as he shook it out. And suddenly—there was Haidee, wearing the dress! Eventually, she had become his partner in the Second Sight Mystery. And for propriety's sake, he had begun to introduce her as his sister.

Back in London now, she found employment—as the clairvoyant in a second-sight act. "Haidee Heller is assisting the celebrated conjuror, Dr. Lynn, at the Piccadilly Hall," reported the *Observer*. But after a while, she quit the act and became the proprietor of a restaurant. Perhaps she had grown weary of performing. Or had not harmonized with Lynn as she had with Heller.

Michael Leavitt, an American theatrical manager, had

---

* At some point Heller seems to have separated from his wife. Not long before his death, a newspaper quoted a claim that Heller had abandoned his wife and children, and that the wife had died of a broken heart. But Heller's father-in-law refuted the charge. His daughter and the children were living in Paris, he said, supported by Heller.

known Haidee professionally. In his memoirs he describes her as "a beautiful and voluptuous looking young English girl." And he tells of running into her at that restaurant:

> Some years after the death of Robert Heller, I entered the Cavour Restaurant, in Leicester Square, London, and was greatly surprised to see Haidee Heller sitting at the cashier's desk with all the composure of being to the manner born. In reply to questions, she told me that she had an interest in the place.

The restaurant was just a few doors from the Alhambra, a popular music hall. So Haidee was probably hobnobbing still with show people.

On March 17, 1893, a notice appeared in the *London Gazette,* reporting the death of "Susannah Jane Ravenhill, otherwise Haidee Heller, otherwise Mrs. Hill." ("Mrs. Hill" must have been a name that she used at the restaurant.) She had died intestate—without a will—it informed any creditors. And it noted that she had never married.

Henry Box Brown

On MAY 2, 1878, HENRY BOX BROWN PERFORMED AT the town hall of Brookline, Massachusetts. The "African Prince" (as he styled himself) was clad in exotic robes, evocative of both Africa and wizardry. His show featured an exposé of spiritualism; a second-sight routine, performed with his wife; and his daughter's escape from a sack. Included also were card tricks, the Enchanted Glass, and the Inexhaustible Hats.

But the highlight of the show was his celebrated box—a wooden crate that he brought out and talked about. This was the very box from which he had emerged thirty years earlier, and that had earned him his nickname. Yet unlike his daughter's escape from the sack (or, years later, Houdini's from the Water Torture Cell), Brown had not escaped *from* this box. Rather, he had escaped *by means of* it—from a life of slavery.

Henry Brown had spent his first 34 years as a slave. He had grown up on a plantation in Virginia called the Hermitage. As a boy he became a household servant. But at fifteen he was bequeathed to his late master's son. This new master brought him to Richmond and put him to work in a tobacco manufactory. In his autobiography Brown describes himself as "the steadiest & swiftest hand in the factory," and the recipient of frequent bonuses. At 21 he married a woman named Nancy. (Unable as slaves to legally marry, they had instead "jumped the broom" together.) They went on to have three children.

Then, in the summer of 1848, Nancy and the children were sold to a minister in North Carolina. Brown tells how he walked alongside the wagon that was taking them away:

> I seized hold of her hand while my mind felt unutterable things, and my tongue was only able to say, we shall meet

in heaven! I went with her for about four miles hand in hand, but both our hearts were so overpowered with feeling that we could say nothing, and when at last we were obliged to part, the look of mutual love which we exchanged was all the token which we could give each other that we should yet meet in heaven.

As Brown mourned his loss, he became estranged from the social order that had sanctioned it. He stopped attending his church, disillusioned with the Christianity of its white leadership. And he began to have "thoughts of freeing myself."

By the spring of 1849 he had come up with a plan to do so. It would require the aid of two acquaintances in Richmond: Samuel Smith, a white shoemaker, and James Smith, a freeman. His escape plan was daring, imaginative, and dangerous. He would have himself shipped to Philadelphia in a box!

The two men agreed to assist him in the scheme; and it was soon underway. Samuel Smith contacted the Anti-

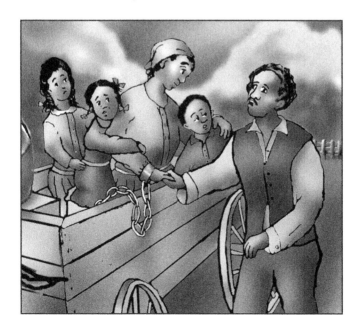

Slavery Society in Philadelphia, and asked them to serve as recipient of the box. The Society's director, J. Miller McKim, hesitated. He feared that Brown might not survive the journey; that the box would prove to be a coffin; and that the Society would be held criminally liable. But how could they refuse to help liberate a slave? Hoping for the best, McKim told Smith to proceed.

A carpenter had been hired to construct the box. His handiwork was now sitting in Smith's shop, ready to go. It was a pinewood crate, similar to those used for shipping dry goods. It measured three feet by two feet by two-and-a-half feet. Smith had lined the interior with canvas and drilled air-holes. Inscribed on the lid was an injunction: "THIS SIDE UP WITH CARE."

On the morning of March 23, Brown climbed into the box. "I laid me down in my darkened home of three feet by two, and like one about to be guillotined, resigned myself to my fate." His supplies for the journey were crackers; a container of water; a gimlet to drill more air-holes; and a hat, for fanning himself. Wishing him well, his accomplices nailed the box shut and sealed it with hickory hoops. And a carter—unaware of what the box contained—drove it to the offices of the Adams Express Company.

Brown's journey, and ordeal, now began. At Adams Express the box was loaded onto a wagon that took it to the rail depot. From there a train transported it as far as the Potomac River. Meanwhile, Samuel Smith was sending a telegram to McKim: "Those goods were shipped this morning & will be in Phila tomorrow morning."

At the river the box was transferred to a steamboat. Four hours later it arrived at the wharf in Washington. A wagon then took it to the B&O rail depot. There it was thrown to the ground, rolled down a declivity (knocking Brown unconscious briefly), and loaded onto a freight car bound for Philadelphia.

Upon reaching the Susquehanna River, the freight cars were ferried across on a barge and re-attached to an engine. And finally, the box arrived at the depot in Philadelphia.

Twenty-seven hours had elapsed since it had been consigned to Adams Express. The company's promise of overnight delivery had been kept.*

The box had been sitting in the depot for less than an hour, when a wagon arrived to pick it up. The driver paid the freight charges—$85—that were due. And the box was driven to the offices of the Anti-Slavery Society and brought inside. There, awaiting the delivery, was J. Miller McKim.

Fearing the worst, McKim approached the box and tapped on it. "All right?" he inquired.

"All right, sir," came a voice from within.

McKim was joined by three other members of the Society. Using a saw and a hatchet, they unsealed the box and removed the lid. And up rose Henry Brown, his face radiant with relief and joy. He was soaked in sweat.

"Good morning, gentlemen," he said, extending his hand.

But Brown was too weak to stand. Instead, he fainted for a moment. Then he climbed out of the box, aided by his welcomers. They congratulated him as he paced about the room, stretching his limbs.

Brown had prepared a hymn to sing, upon gaining his freedom. The four men fell silent as he sang its opening verse:

> *I waited patiently, I waited patiently*
> *for the Lord, for the Lord*
> *And he inclined unto me*
> *and heard my calling.*

---

* Its agents had failed, however, to scrupulously observe the injunction of "THIS SIDE UP." Several times Brown found himself upside down. The first time, he was able to shift himself into an upright position. But the second time, on the steamboat, he was fearful of being heard by the passengers, and resolved to endure the physical distress. To his relief, two passengers righted the box. They then sat down on it and talked. It would have surprised them to learn that their conversation was being overheard by the contents of the box.

But he was too weak to go on. It was decided that any further ceremony could wait. McKim escorted Brown from the offices, and took him home for a bath and a meal.

•

Henry Box Brown (as he became known) began his new life. The Anti-Slavery Society had sought to keep secret the story of his escape; for as a runaway slave, Brown was subject to arrest. Furthermore, they did not want to jeopardize for others this innovative means of escape. But the tale was too good to go untold; and it spread. By the end of April, the story was appearing in newspapers. And by June, Brown was being asked to speak at abolitionist meetings.

Initially, he had found a place to live in New Bedford. With its anti-slavery sentiment, and distance from the South, the New England town was a safe place for a runaway. Moreover, one of his sisters lived there, as did several persons known to him from Richmond. But after speaking, and singing his hymn of thanksgiving, at an anti-slavery rally in Boston, he moved to that city. There he was launched by activists on what would become his career as an anti-slavery lecturer.

Speaking in meeting halls, he described his years of bondage and his daring escape. His lectures were well-attended; for Brown's feat had become famous. Moreover, he spoke "with a simple, earnest, and unadorned eloquence," according to one review. And after the first year, he added something that drew even larger audiences: a moving panorama.

Moving panoramas were a popular attraction of the day. (A dozen of them were currently being exhibited in London.) Meant to be both entertaining and edifying, they were a nineteenth-century version of the slide show. On a long canvas a succession of scenes were painted. The canvas was attached to rollers, like a scroll, and to pulleys. As it was wound along, the scenes unfolded before the audience. Meanwhile, the exhibitor commented on them; and a pianist provided music. Most of the panoramas were travelogues, such as *Panorama of the Mississippi River.* (It was advertised, à la Barnum, as being three miles long!) Some, like *Panorama of the Bible* ("over a mile in length"), were historical.

Brown's panorama had been painted by a team of artists in Boston. It was 600 feet long and consisted of 49 scenes. Titled *Mirror of Slavery*, it depicted the history and iniquities of American slavery. Shown were scenes of the slave trade; of the lives of slaves on a plantation; and of escapes, including his own. Brown narrated the scenes as they came into view. In addition, he sang his hymn and other songs; exhibited the box that had been his means of escape; and sold copies of the *Narrative of Henry Box Brown*—an autobiography that Brown (who could neither read nor write) had produced with the aid of a ghostwriter.*

As he toured New England with his panorama, he was assisted by James Smith, the freeman who had helped him to escape. James Smith had fled Richmond and joined Brown. As for Samuel Smith, the other accomplice, he proved less fortunate. Attempting to liberate two more slaves via Adams Express, he was discovered; tried and found

---

* The ghostwriter was Charles Stearns, a radical abolitionist and pamphleteer who advocated Dis-Union—the idea that the North should dissolve its connection with the South. The full title of the 92-page book was *Narrative of Henry Box Brown, Who Escaped from Slavery Enclosed in a Box 3 Feet Long and 2 Wide. Written from a Statement of Facts Made by Himself. With Remarks upon the Remedy for Slavery.* Included were a portrait of Brown, the text of his "Hymn of Thanksgiving," and a picture of the box. Published in September 1849, the book sold well; and Brown used the profits to help pay for the panorama.

The book tells the tale of Brown's early years. Two years later, a rewritten version—with less florid prose—would be published. The *Narrative* is a moving document. And for a painstakingly researched account of his entire life, see *The Unboxing of Henry Brown* by Jeffrey Ruggles (2003), which has served as my main source of information about Brown.

guilty; and sentenced to six-and-a-half years in prison.*

A unique kind of showman—one with both a moving panorama and a message—Brown appeared in the same halls as other entertainers and lecturers. And he continued to attract large, and paying, audiences. He was living frugally and saving his money, in hope of purchasing the freedom of his wife and children. But then, in September 1850, Congress passed the Fugitive Slave Act. The law required that an escaped slave be returned to his owner. And Brown found himself on the run.

●

An earlier Fugitive Slave Act had become law in 1793. It was of little consequence in the free states: local officials simply refused to enforce it. But the new version—part of a compromise between the North and the South (in return, California would be admitted to the Union as a free state) —called for strict enforcement, by both federal and local officials. Many in the North were incensed; for even private citizens would now be obliged to aid in the capture of runaways.

On the eve of the passage of the law, an attempt had been made to abduct Brown. He was walking down Broad Street in Providence, when several men set upon him. They beat him and attempted to drag him into a carriage. He fought them off and fled.

Brown was the most public—and provocative—of escaped

---

* Upon his release, Samuel Smith was aided financially by the Anti-Slavery Society. In *The Underground Rail Road* (1872), William Still, one of the four men present when Brown emerged from the box, says of Smith: "After being united in marriage...to a lady who had remained faithful to him through all his sore trials and sufferings, he took his departure for Western New York, with a good conscience and an unshaken faith in the belief that in aiding his fellow-man to freedom he had but simply obeyed the word of Him who taught man to do unto others as he would be done by."

slaves; and he was being targeted by slave catchers. Immediately, he went into hiding. Friends advised him to leave the country. And a few weeks later, he boarded a ship that was bound for Liverpool. Accompanying him was James Smith. Brown was carrying letters of introduction, from American abolitionists to their counterparts in Great Britain. With him too was the *Mirror of Slavery*.

Soon after his arrival, he began exhibiting the panorama in Liverpool. After a month there, he took it on tour. Antislavery sentiment in Britain was strong; and Brown drew large audiences wherever he went. Moreover, he was becoming an astute showman. As an opening act he had engaged a trio of opera singers. And his ads promised an evening's entertainment, despite the grimness of the subject matter. Nor was he adverse to publicity stunts. Adopting exotic garb and calling himself "the African Prince," he paraded through streets in front of a brass band. And for an engagement in Leeds, he took the train from nearby Bradford—enclosed in his famous box. Along with his ads, local newspapers ran reviews of the show.

For 25 years Henry Box Brown would reside in Great Britain. During most of that period he exhibited the *Mirror of Slavery*. But new scenes—of the Holy Land—were added to it. And he commissioned two additional panoramas: one of the war in India, the other of the American Civil War. He had become a full-fledged showman—an exhibitor of panoramas. And he was still narrating them, singing, displaying his box, and selling copies of his book.

As for his personal life, he had parted ways with James Smith; the two had quarreled over money. And he had despaired of ever being reunited with his wife and children. (Or perhaps they seemed part of a life, or of an identity, that he had left behind.) For he married an Englishwoman, who became his assistant in the show.

As he traveled from town to town, Brown met other entertainers who followed the same circuit. One of these joined his show: Professor Chadwick, the hypnotist. But Brown soon let Chadwick go and took his place. Advertising

himself as "the King of All Mesmerists," he hypnotized audience members and lectured on "electro-biology." It was the beginning of his transformation into a magician. He began to add magic tricks to the show. And eventually, he would retire the panoramas (the form was rendered obsolete by photography); bill himself as Professor H. Box Brown; and entertain solely as a magician.

●

In 1875 he returned to the U.S., with his wife and daughter. In some of the same halls where he had campaigned against slavery, he now performed as a magician. In the years that followed, Brown traveled about New England, publicizing his show with handbills and eking out a living. Little is known, however, of this final phase of his life—not even when he died or where he is buried.

Brown's performance at the town hall of Brookline is one of the few of which a record has been found. It included mindreading, an exposé of spiritualism, and his daughter's escape from a sack. And he was still exhibiting his box.

The box belonged in the show. As a Philadelphia minister, addressing a meeting of the Anti-Slavery Society, had declared:

> A slave, worth a few hundred dollars, was put into a box. The box was nailed down; and, after being well shaken, and turned over a number of times, it was opened, and out leaped a freeman, whose value no man can compute. That box has magic in it.

Bellachini

SAMUEL BERLACH (1828–1885) GREW UP IN LIGOTA, POLAND, the son of a Jewish innkeeper. As a youth he tried to learn carpentry, but lacked the aptitude and temperament for such work. What he did not lack was a spirit of adventure. So with $10 from his father, Samuel made his way to London. From there he worked his way across the Atlantic as a cabin-boy.

Disappointed with America, Samuel sailed back to Europe —this time as a stowaway. From Lisbon he set out on foot for home. On the way, however, he fell in with a band of Gypsies. He lived and traveled with them. And he found his calling. For a Gypsy taught him the art of legerdemain; and Samuel was soon performing at fairs and marketplaces.

Such were his rude beginnings as a conjurer. As his skills improved, he acquired paraphernalia and worked up a stage act. And under the name "Bellachini," he became a popular entertainer, appearing at cafes, hotels, and theatres throughout Germany. His success enabled him to marry the daughter of a prominent physician.

His show was titled *Aegyptische Magie.* It featured the latest mechanical and electrical illusions. As a performer, Bellachini was only moderately competent at sleight of hand. His strength lay in his comedic abilities, his stage presence, and his jovial manner. An example of his jocularity: he would sometimes come on stage as if having just arrived at the theatre. Removing his overcoat and gloves, he began the show by saying (in his broken German): "Unprepared as I am…"

A highlight of the show was his famous egg trick. Bellachini made an egg vanish. Then he approached his assistant, who was standing off to the side as if awaiting a command. He pressed on the assistant's belly—causing an egg to emerge from the man's mouth. As Bellachini

pressed again and again on his belly, eggs kept emerging from the assistant's mouth. Audiences found it hilarious.

Bellachini became Germany's best-known magician. His career peaked when Emperor Wilhelm appointed him *Hofzauberkünstler,* or Court Conjurer. According to the London *Telegraph,* Bellachini used a magic trick to obtain this appointment:

> Signor Bellachini, the renowned prestidigitator, who has recently been honoured by the German Emperor with the complimentary title of "Royal Court Artist," obtained this unprecedented distinction by a somewhat remarkable feat of dexterity.
>
> Having observed that the venerable monarch for some years past frequently attended his performances and exhibited a lively interest in the magical arts of which he is a Past

Master, Bellachini conceived the bold project of turning imperial favour to account, and made formal application to His Majesty for an audience. His petition was granted, and the Emperor received him at an appointed hour in the study overlooking the Linden avenue, his favourite room, in which he transacts business every morning and after-noon.

After chatting for a few minutes with the accomplished conjurer upon subjects connected with his profession, [the Emperor] asked, with a smile, "Well, Bellachini, and what is it you want of me?"

"It is my most humble request, Sire, that Your Majesty would deign to appoint me your Court Artist."

"I will do so, Bellachini, but upon one consideration only —namely, that you forthwith perform some extraordinarily clever trick, worthy of the favour you solicit."

Without a moment's hesitation, Bellachini took up a pen from the Emperor's inkstand, handed it with a sheet of paper to His Majesty, and requested him to write the words: "Bellachini can do nothing at all."

The Emperor attempted to comply, but, strange to say, neither pen nor ink could be persuaded to fulfill their functions.

"Now, Sire," said Bellachini, "will Your Majesty condescend to write the words 'Bellachini is the Emperor's Court Artist'?"

The second attempt was as successful as the first had been the contrary; pen, ink and paper, delivered from the spell cast over them by the magician, proved perfectly docile to the imperial hand, and Bellachini's ingenious trick was rewarded on the spot by his nomination to the desired honorific office, made out in the Emperor's own writing.

Henry Slade

ENRY SLADE GREW UP ON A FARM IN JOHNSON CREEK, a hamlet about thirty miles from Niagara Falls. When he was twenty, he left home and headed west. He wound up in Albion, a small town in southern Michigan with a train station and a college. Years later, Dr. Slade (as he was calling himself) would be remembered:

> In the year 1855 when this writer was a clerk in S. Tuttle & Son's drug store in Albion, there came to reside in the village a young man, who claimed to be a spiritual doctor. He was well dressed, very affable and soon became quite well known....Our acquaintance grew quite intimate as he purchased all of his drugs and medicines at the store where I was employed. Occasionally he gave demonstrations of his spirit rappings, slate writings, moving of tables, etc. that seemed quite miraculous. (Elmore Palmer, "Biographical Sketches," 1908)

The newcomer offered his services as a "spiritual doctor" —a practitioner with both psychic powers and a knowledge of medicinal plants. He would enter a trance; contact the spirit world; and with the aid of a spirit, make his diagnosis. His psychic powers had apparently been with him since boyhood. As for his knowledge of plants, perhaps it had been acquired from the Indians who still dwelt in the vicinity of Johnson Creek. (In the 1860 census, Slade would list his profession as "Indian doctor.")

Three years after coming to Albion, he married Emily Bradley; and they moved to the nearby town of Jackson. There Slade continued to practice his occult brand of medicine. But he had also fallen in with Spiritualists. And at some point he became a medium—an intermediary between the living and the dead.

He began to travel about, in Michigan and beyond, conducting séances. In 1863 he conducted one at the home of Gardiner Knapp, in New Albany, Indiana. During this séance Slade introduced an innovation that would bring him fame among Spiritualists—and notoriety among skeptics. It involved a tablet-sized slate, like the ones used in schools. Mediums used such slates to record the messages they received from spirits. The medium would enter a trance; connect with a spirit guide (or "control"); and begin to write on the slate. This was called "automatic writing." (The Ouija board is a popularized form of it.) But Slade went further. In what became known as "independent slate writing," he would summon a spirit—*and the spirit itself would write on the slate.*

The *Banner of Light* was a Spiritualist newspaper, published in Boston. In April 1866 it printed a letter describing one of Slade's séances:

> Dr. Slade, of Jackson, Michigan, has been here for a few days, giving such overwhelming proofs of spirit-existence and power as to disarm the veriest skeptic. I had the satisfaction of attending one of his seances. In a gas-lighted room, we heard the raps, loud and frequent, under the table and on the back of the medium's chair. Then, a tiny piece of slate pencil so small that no mortal writer could make use of it, was placed on a slate, and the medium held it [the slate] under the table with one hand, his other hand resting on the table, where all our hands were also placed. We heard the scratching of the pencil over the slate, and three little taps announced that the writing was completed.

Slade brought the slate out from under the table. And to the amazement of all, names were written on it—left there by the spirit! Slade then held a small accordion under the table with one hand. His ghostly visitor took hold of the keyboard end; and together they played "Home, Sweet Home." The tune was played with such feeling, says the letter-writer, "that brought tears to my eyes, and I hope the joyous certainty of eternal life and happiness to other hearts."

Alas, the medium himself was in need of such consolation. For the year before, his wife Emily had died, at the age of 26. Slade was still grieving, as he went on conducting séances and practicing medicine.

In January 1868 he remarried. His new wife, Dr. Alcinda Wilhelm, M.D., was one of the first women to have attended a medical school. She was also a Spiritualist of note. Dr. Wilhelm had been touring as an "inspirational speaker," lecturing on Spiritualism and women's rights. Now she and Slade started a joint medical practice, in Kalamazoo, that included clairvoyant diagnosis and magnetic remedies.

A year later, after an illness, Alcinda too died. For many months Slade was inconsolable. Finally, he left Michigan, moving first to Boston, then to New York.

●

During the next five years, Henry Slade conducted his séances primarily in New York. He seems to have put medicine aside and become a full-time medium. So astonishing were his manifestations that his services—rendered for a fee—were in constant demand. His fame grew; and Slade prospered.

Conducted in full light, the sessions were held for one or two sitters at a time. Trembling and twitching, Slade would enter a trance. He then summoned one of his spirit guides. And uncanny events began to occur. One never knew what would happen next. A chair was knocked over by the spirit. Or mysterious raps were heard. Or the table rose from the floor. Or beneath the table, the spirit pinched the sitter.

But the high point of the séance—the tour de force for which Slade had become famous—was the slate-writing. There were various forms of it. In one, a pair of slates were shown to be blank. They were tied together securely and kept in full view on the table. When they were untied, a lengthy message (often in response to a question) was revealed—left there by the spirit. In another, a single slate was held under the table. A scratching sound was heard. And a message was found scrawled on the slate. Conveyed by the spirit guide, these messages came from departed souls.

Slade had three spirit guides whom he regularly summoned. One was an Indian named Owasso. Another was Dr. Davis, a healer. But the guide most frequently summoned was "Allie," as he called her—Alcinda, his late wife. This invisible spirit conveyed messages from the departed. She made rapping sounds and sent chairs flying. And on one memorable occasion, *Alcinda materialized in the séance room.*

It happened during the winter of 1875, when Slade was at the height of his fame. Emma Hardinge, a prominent Spiritualist, had dropped by his New York apartment, along with two of her friends. Their intent was merely to pay a social call. But when Slade offered them an impromptu sitting, the women accepted the offer.

Slade sat them in his séance room. He lit a pair of lamps; hung a black sheet with a square hole cut in it; and intimated that a materialization might be in the offing. And they were chatting amicably, when one of Hardinge's friends whispered to her, in an awe-struck tone: "Look there!"

I turned my head and perceived behind me, but quite far away from Mr. Slade, a column of white mist, shapeless, and with the particles moving like smoke, but very white and luminous. Directly I turned my head this misty mass moved swiftly behind my chair, and disappeared at the black screen. The muslin was so thin that we could see the wall through it, and see, also, something like circling smoke moving behind it. Before I could have counted a hundred, there appeared at the square opening, directly behind Mr. Slade's head, the face of my dear friend, Dr. Alcinda Wilhelm—a lady with whom I had once been very intimate—who had subsequently become Mr. Slade's wife, and who is now one of his principal controlling spirits. This dear and well-known face could not be mistaken. She wore her hair in the peculiar curls that I so well remembered, though they were not then in fashion, and on her head was a bridal wreath, about which she and I had had some conversation before her marriage. My two friends recognised Alcinda Wilhelm as clearly as I did; but Mr. Slade, who seemed very nervous, did not turn his head to look at her until she had gradually melted into the indistinct white mist. (Emma Hardinge, "Dark Circles and Cabinets," 1882)

That same year, Madame Blavatsky, the founder of Theosophy, received a request from the Russian government. They wanted her to select a medium who was skilled at manifestations. He would come to St. Petersburg and be subjected to scientific testing. A thousand dollars would be paid, to cover his expenses.

Blavatsky was residing in New York at the time and may have known Slade personally. In any case, he was the most celebrated medium in the country. She selected him to receive the thousand dollars.

And in January 1876, Henry Slade—accompanied by his assistant, his niece, and the assistant's daughter—boarded a ship, bound for Liverpool.

●

London was intended merely as a stopover en route to Russia. But Slade knew there were many Spiritualists in the city. And seeing an opportunity to further his career, he decided to stay for a while. He found lodgings in Russell Square and began to conduct séances.

One of his first sitters was a reporter from the *World*, who found Slade's physical appearance distinctive:

A highly-wrought, nervous temperament, a dreamy, mystical face, regular features, eyes luminous with expression, a rather sad smile, and a certain melancholy grace of manner, were the impressions conveyed by the tall, lithe figure introduced to me as Dr. Slade. He is the sort of man you would pick out of a roomful as an enthusiast [religious visionary].

Henry Slade was soon the talk of the town. In *The History of Spiritualism*, Arthur Conan Doyle recalls that "his success was immediate and pronounced." Prominent Spiritualists scheduled sittings with him. They witnessed his manifestations, under test conditions, and strongly endorsed him. "We have no hesitation in saying," declared the editor of *Spiritual Magazine*, "that Dr. Slade is the most remarkable medium of modern times."

Yet many Londoners were skeptical, and believed Slade to be a fraud. Among them was Ray Lankester, professor of zoology at University College London. An outspoken materialist, Lankester was a pugnacious apostle for the gospel of science, and a sworn enemy of Spiritualism. Appalled by the adulation that Slade was receiving, he set out to expose him.

Accompanied by a colleague, Lankester came in for a sitting. At a crucial point he leapt up and snatched the slate out of Slade's hands. Supposedly blank (the spirit had not yet begun to write), it contained a lengthy message. And when Slade tried to shake something out of his hand, Lankester caught it—a thimble with a bit of slate pencil attached. Accusations and protestations were exchanged; and the sitting ended in an uproar.

Triumphant, Lankester wrote a letter to the *Times*, accusing Slade of being a fraud. The letter was published and widely read, sparking a controversy. And Lankester went further: he pressed charges against Slade.

Slade was arrested, along with Simmons, his assistant. They were charged with obtaining money under false pretenses. Or in the legal parlance of the Vagrancy Act, "unlawfully using certain subtle and crafty means and devices to deceive."

Their trial began on October 1, 1876, in the Bow Street Police Court. Such was public interest in the case that the courtroom was filled to overflowing. Crowded together were both supporters and detractors of Slade, along with a pack of journalists. The *Times* published a daily transcript of the proceedings.

The principal witness for the prosecution was Lankester. A corpulent, bearlike man, he filled the witness box. Lankester described grabbing a slate that was supposedly empty, and finding it filled with writing. He claimed that Slade had used sleight of hand to exchange slates. Asked if he had actually observed this sleight of hand, Lankester admitted that he had not. "The nature of sleight of hand— if there is sleight of hand—prevents you observing," he explained. Laughter filled the courtroom, as it would often during the trial. Lankester's testimony was confirmed by the colleague who had accompanied him.

Another witness was a magazine editor named Hutton. During an earlier séance, Hutton testified, he had proposed a test: have the spirit leave a message inside a double slate that has been fastened with a lock. But Slade had declined the test, claiming that his wife's spirit refused to write on locked slates. When Hutton asked if some other spirit might be willing to do so, Slade had checked with the spirits. Their response, found scrawled on a slate, was emphatic: "NOT ONE WORD."

But the most compelling, and entertaining, testimony was provided by John Nevil Maskelyne, England's foremost magician. The prosecutor had told the court: "You will find that nothing that Slade does is at all beyond the power of any ordinary conjurer." And he had called on Maskelyne to reproduce Slade's miracles by non-supernatural means. Maskelyne had stepped into the witness box and put on a magic show. He demonstrated techniques by which writing could seemingly be elicited from a spirit. In one example he used a thimble device to surreptitiously write on a slate. The slate was handed up to the judge, who read aloud (with mock amazement): "'The spirits are present.'"

Maskelyne was enjoying the opportunity to perform, with the spectators as audience. He was also relishing his role as expert witness. At one point the séance table was carried into the courtroom, amid laughter; and Maskelyne was asked to examine it. It was an ordinary kitchen table, with four legs, two flaps, and a bracket. Maskelyne examined it. "It is a very remarkable table," he said, in a tone that provoked still more merriment.

Slade's defense had become a cause célèbre among Spiritualists. They had raised money for a Defense Fund and provided him with a lawyer. Eminent Spiritualists had agreed to testify in his behalf. One of them was Alfred Russel Wallace, the naturalist who had co-discovered with Darwin the principle of natural selection. He and Darwin had since parted ways, with Wallace—convinced that the ultimate aim of evolution was the creation of immortal souls —becoming a Spiritualist.

Wallace now took the stand, as a witness for the defense. He described his own sitting with Slade. During it Wallace had received messages on slates; heard raps; felt a spirit touch his leg; and observed the table levitate. There was no doubt in his mind that these phenomena had been real and that Slade was genuine. From beginning to end, he insisted, he had seen "nothing whatever indicative of imposture."

Three other Spiritualists—equally eminent—took the stand. They testified as to Slade's integrity and his powers as a medium. For all its absurdity, the trial had become an intellectual battleground—an encounter between Spiritualists and materialists. Even Darwin had joined the fray, sending Lankester a letter of support.

When the testimonies had concluded, the judge delivered his verdict. He rejected as irrelevant Maskelyne's conjuring demonstrations. The fact that such techniques *could* have been used did not prove that they had been. He ignored too the testimony, by Wallace and the other Spiritualists, that Slade had previously displayed genuine powers:

What is before the Court is not what has happened upon other occasions—however convincing these eminent witnesses may be—but what occurred upon this particular occasion, and here we have two witnesses on one side and only the prisoner on the other.

His decision was necessarily based, said the judge, on "inferences to be drawn from the known course of nature." And finding Slade guilty of deception, he sentenced him to three months imprisonment with hard labor.

Slade appealed the decision and was released on bail. In January the appeal was heard; and the conviction was overturned—on a technicality. The words "by palmistry or otherwise," which appeared in the statute, had inadvertently been omitted from the indictment.

Determined that Slade should be jailed ("in the interest of science"), Lankester obtained a fresh summons against him. But Slade was already gone. He and his entourage had fled to France.

●

In an open letter signed by forty-nine Spiritualists, and published in *Spiritual Magazine*, the persecution of Slade was decried:

> In view of the deplorable termination of Henry Slade's visit to this country, WE the undersigned desire to place on record our high opinion of his MEDIUMSHIP, and our reprobation of the treatment he has undergone....We unhesitatingly avow our high appreciation of Henry Slade's powers as a MEDIUM, our sympathy with him in the great anxiety and distress which he has undergone, and our unshaken confidence in his integrity.

And his flight to France was given a positive spin:

> His Defence Committee have, therefore, on their sole responsibility, advised him to decline the further jurisdiction of English law courts, it being their opinion that every claim of honour has been already satisfied.

But his reputation had suffered a blow. And in France he received a hostile reception. Lankester had made sure of that, contacting French newspapers and informing them of the fraud conviction. Because of the hostility, Slade moved on—to Belgium and Holland, conducting séances as he went. His ultimate destination was still Russia, where testing awaited him.

By November Slade and his companions had gotten as far east as Berlin. There they stayed at the Kronprinz Hotel. Slade conducted a séance for the hotel's owner; and word spread of his powers. Soon, his services as a medium were in demand. As in London, prominent persons showed up for a sitting. So too did the chief of police. Impressed with the results, he did not interfere with Slade.

Slade's genuineness was debated. Was he really in touch with spirits? Or were his manifestations nothing more than conjuring tricks? It was decided that an expert opinion was needed. And who better to render such an opinion than the Emperor's own conjurer? Bellachini was contacted and asked to test Slade. He agreed to do so.

For a week he paid daily visits to Slade's hotel room. Diligently, he observed the slate-writing, the accordion-playing, and other marvels. Bellachini was familiar with the tricks of his trade, and kept an eye out for them.

Finally, he issued an affidavit:

After I had, at the wish of several highly-esteemed gentlemen of rank and position, and also for my own interest, tested the physical mediumship of Mr. Slade in a series of sittings by full daylight, as well as in the evening, in his bedroom, I must, for the sake of truth, hereby certify that the phenomenal occurrences with Mr. Slade have been thoroughly examined by me with the minutest observation and investigation of his surroundings, including the table, and that I have *not in the smallest degree* found anything to be produced by means of prestidigitative manifestations, or by mechanical apparatus; and that any explanation of the experiments which took place *under the circumstances and*

conditions then obtaining by any reference to prestidigita-
tion *is absolutely* impossible.

Slade's powers were real, declared Bellachini in a signed
and notarized statement. Or at least, he could find no evidence of trickery. He added that it was up to men of science
"to search for an explanation of this phenomenal power, and
to prove its reality."

As it turned out, a man of science was eager to do so, and
had been awaiting Bellachini's verdict. If Slade's powers
were deemed to be real, this scientist wanted to verify their
existence under strict conditions—that is to say, scientifi-
cally. His name was Zöllner.

Johann Karl Friedrich Zöllner was a distinguished
astronomer. He held the position of Professor of Astronomy
and Physics at the University of Leipzig. His *On the Nature
of Comets* (1872) was the definitive work on the subject.
Professor Zöllner had also made a study of optical illusions.
(He originated what is known as the Zöllner illusion, in
which parallel lines appear to diverge.) And he was a theo-
rist of non-Euclidean geometry. Zöllner was convinced that
space had a fourth dimension. Invisible to the human eye,
he believed, was an entire world—a four-dimensional
realm. And inhabiting it were intelligent beings.

Zöllner's theory had led him to an interest in Spiritualism. The spirit world, he came to believe, was that four-
dimensional realm; and the spirits were those intelligent
beings. Thus, he saw in Henry Slade a unique opportunity.
The American medium might be the key to proving his
theory. Zöllner had already held an informal session with
Slade; and the results had been encouraging. Now that
Slade had been deemed genuine, Zöllner wanted to test his
powers in a controlled environment.

Zöllner got in touch with Slade. Would he be willing to
come to Leipzig and undergo a series of tests? He would be
remunerated, of course, for his time and effort. Though
busy with sittings, Slade agreed to be tested.

The testing began in mid December and continued for

eight days. Three other scientists from the university were present, acting as witnesses: Professor Fechner (a physicist), Professor Scheibner (a mathematician), and Professor Weber (a physicist). Everyone sat at a table in Zöllner's study. And Slade's powers were tested.*

Initially, Zöllner had sought to impose upon him a rigid set of conditions. But manifestations had failed to occur; and it became clear that the conditions were inhibiting Slade and interfering with his powers. He did receive one message: the spirits were requesting less rigid conditions. So he was allowed to proceed in his usual way, though under close scrutiny.

And manifestations began to occur. Messages appeared on slates. Raps were heard. A compass needle swayed violently. A spectral hand was glimpsed at the edge of the table. A bell, placed beneath the table, rang. And a chair was levitated, along with its occupant: an astonished Professor Fechner.

Then came a series of challenges that Zöllner had specially designed. One of these involved a rope. Its two ends were joined together and sealed with wax. Could the spirits tie a knot in this loop, asked Zöllner, without disturbing the seal? (He thought their four-dimensional nature might allow them to do so.) On an earlier attempt, nothing had happened. But the experiment was repeated—with startling results. Slade held the rope beneath the table and sum-

---

* Zöllner's critics insisted that the four professors were incapable of detecting the trickery of a skilled conjurer. Zöllner, they claimed, was of unsound mind; Fechner was nearly blind; Scheibner had poor eyesight; and Weber was doddering with age. But according to Joseph Cook, an American clergyman who traveled to Leipzig and met with him, the charges against Zöllner were untrue. "His predominant expression in face and bearing is that of a cheerful, enthusiastic, and incisive intellectual courage. He impresses you at once as a man of mental power, and also as one of geniality and social warmth."

Of course, the fact remains: a skilled conjurer can fool anyone.

moned a spirit. When he withdrew it, four knots were found tied in the rope.

The eight days of testing concluded; and Zöllner announced his findings. Henry Slade did indeed have remarkable powers. They enabled him to communicate with "spirits"—that is to say, with beings from a higher plane of existence. Moreover, Slade could induce these beings to manifest their presence, in a variety of ways. Three of his colleagues had witnessed these phenomena, said Zöllner; and all had agreed that Slade's powers were real.*

Zöllner would publish an account of his sessions with Slade, along with an exposition of his theory of four-dimensional space. In *Transcendental Physics* he tells of "a new class of physical phenomena which proclaim to astonished mankind, with assurance no longer doubted, the existence of another material and intelligent world." He assures the reader that "all the manifestations were given in the light and under circumstances which utterly precluded the slightest possibility of fraud or deception." And he describes Slade's reaction to the investigation of "his peculiar endowments":

> He expressed in warm terms his happiness that he had, for the first time, succeeded in interesting men of sincere inclination to truth...in such a degree that they had resolved to institute scientific experiments with him.

----

* Or had they? According to magician Peter Lamont, Zöllner viewed the appearance of knots in the rope as conclusive evidence for the existence of a fourth dimension. "He wrote to Fechner, who had attended previous séances, and who had been unsure whether Slade was genuine or not. Fechner agreed that, *if* it were not a trick [emphasis added], this would indeed be strong evidence. Zöllner, convinced that it was not a trick, then claimed that Fechner agreed with him, and the authenticity of the spirit knots was subsequently announced, supported by the considerable clout of Fechner's scientific credentials." ("Henry Slade and the Fourth Dimension," *Genii*, June 2009)

•

Finally he arrived in St. Petersburg, for testing at the Imperial University. Before it began, he held a sitting for the Grand Duke Constantine, brother of the Tsar. A message appeared on a slate that the Grand Duke was holding. Amazed, he acclaimed Slade's powers. Less impressed were the scientists who subsequently tested Slade. They detected trickery and sent him packing.

Undaunted, he returned to Leipzig, where Zöllner conducted further tests. Then he went back to London. After a brief stay (during which he kept a low profile, fearing re-arrest), he sailed to Australia.

Slade remained in Australia for several months, conducting séances and causing a stir. But he was growing homesick. And in the summer of 1879, he sailed to San Francisco. After a stay in Colorado, he returned to New York; found lodgings; and advertised that his services were once again available.

•

Throughout the next decade, Slade was able to support himself as a medium. He also lectured on Spiritualism. But the rage for séances had subsided; and his services were less in demand. Moreover, his reputation had suffered additional blows. The worst of them had come from the Seybert Commission.

Funded by a bequest in the will of a Spiritualist (by a spirit, as it were!), the Seybert Commission had been established at the University of Pennsylvania. Its mission was to make a systematic study of the phenomenon of Spiritualism. Slade and other mediums were paid $300 each, to conduct séances under the observation of the members of the Commission.*

---

* One of the members was Dr. Silas Weir Mitchell, son of the final owner of Maelzel's Chess-Player. Having been privy to the inner workings of the Turk, he may have been particularly alert to fakery.

When their report was issued, Slade (along with the other mediums) was declared to be fraudulent. The report referred to "several little tricks which he imputed to Spiritual agency, but which were almost puerile in the simplicity of their legerdemain." One commissioner found him to be particularly offensive:

> The methods of this Medium's operations appear to me to be perfectly transparent, and I wish to say emphatically that I am astonished beyond expression at the confidence of this man in his ability to deceive, and at the recklessness of the risks which he assumes in his deceptions, which are practiced in the most barefaced manner.

In his remarks on Slade, the chairman of the Commission decried the trickery that had been detected (though he confessed that one trick "was so clever I wanted to applaud him on the spot"). And he described Slade:

> He is probably six feet in height….His face would, I think, attract notice anywhere for its uncommon beauty. He has a small, curling, dark moustache, and short, crisp, iron-grey hair, of a texture exceeding in fineness any that I have ever seen on a man's head. His eyes are dark, and the circles around them very dark, but their expression is painful. I could not divest myself of the feeling that it was that of a hunted animal or of a haunted man.

The chairman added that he had dined with Slade on several occasions and found him to be affable. And more recently, he had run into Slade in Boston. "Well, and how are the old Spirits coming on?" he had asked the medium. Slade had laughed and replied: "Oh, pshaw! You never believed in them, did you?"

Not long after his séances for the Seybert Commission, Slade conducted one in Weston, West Virginia—and was caught faking the manifestations. A complaint was filed; and he was arrested, along with his assistant Simmons.

Released on bail, they grabbed their bags and left town in a hurry (with no intention of returning). But the damage was done. The story was reported in the local newspaper and widely reprinted. A townsman was quoted as saying: "I believe him to be a double-dyed scoundrel of the basest character."

Slade insisted that it had all been a mistake. But he apparently thought it best to put some distance between himself and the adverse publicity. For in 1886 he returned to England—under the name "Dr. Wilson"—and to Germany. In Hamburg he held a sitting with a magician named Willmann, who kept a sharp eye on his every move. "Slade was unable to distract my attention from the crucial point of the trick," reports Willmann, "and threw down the slates on the table in disgust, remarking: 'I cannot obtain any results today, the power that controls me is exhausted. Come tomorrow.'" But the next day, Slade was unavailable.

The following year he was back in New York, residing in a boarding house on East Ninth Street. His niece played piano during the sittings that were held there. But Henry Slade was in decline, both professionally and physically. He was in ill health, having suffered a stroke. And he was drinking. Arthur Conan Doyle, a believer in Slade's powers, attributes his use of trickery to this decline:

> There is ample evidence that Slade degenerated in general character towards the latter part of his life. Promiscuous sittings with a mercenary object, the subsequent exhaustions, and the alcoholic stimulus which affords a temporary relief, all acting upon a most sensitive organisation, had a deleterious effect. This weakening of character, with a corresponding loss of health, may have led to a diminution of his psychic powers, and increased the temptation to resort to trickery.

Despite his ills, he continued to ply his trade. This notice appeared in the Glens Falls *Morning Star* for September 7, 1895:

HE HAS ARRIVED

Dr. Henry Slade, of New York, the world-renowned independent slate writing medium, will give private sittings for independent slate writing at the American house. Engagements for sittings should be made in advance. The doctor will examine, in a clairvoyant state, the sick free of charge.

And five years later, Stanley Krebs, an investigating psychologist, found him plying his trade at a summer resort. Slade had rented a cottage and hung out his shingle. Krebs engaged a sitting. For two dollars he received a lengthy message (with generic advice) from the spirit of Dr. Davis. A small mirror, hidden in his lap, enabled Krebs to see under the table. There he observed an inscribed slate being substituted for the blank one.

Slade died in 1905. In an obituary, the *Brooklyn Daily Eagle* described his final days:

> He went West and showed up at last in Detroit. There he lived, old, broken, and half insane, in one room, and made his living by giving "tests" to servant girls for 10 cents a sitting. In time he got too broken even for that and was sent to a sanatorium, where he died.

He is buried in Albion, beside Emma, his first wife. A monument, erected by Spiritualists, marks the grave.

•

To produce his manifestations—the slate-writing, the mysterious raps, the jumping chairs—Henry Slade employed the skills and techniques of a conjurer. He *was* a conjurer— one who pretended to have mediumistic powers. But how exactly did he do it? How did he produce those manifestations? How did he create the illusion that a spirit was causing them?

Slate-writing became a standard effect in the repertoire of fake mediums. But Henry Slade originated it and made it the centerpiece of his séances. Typically, he would hold the slate, with one hand, against the underside of the table —to "develop power," away from the light. On his finger was that thimble device (known in the trade as a "nail writer"); and with it he surreptitiously wrote on the slate. But he could also produce a message on slates that were kept in plain sight. He had a variety of methods for doing so: removable flaps, invisible ink, sleight-of-hand substitutions. And he was a master of misdirection.*

Many of his other manifestations were made possible by a rare physical endowment. Slade had a "rubber leg," as it was called. His long legs had a flexibility—an agility—that rivaled that of his arms. With them he could reach anywhere under the table. He could move chairs—slap legs— throw things—make rapping sounds—tug on clothing (grasping it with his toes). Krebs even saw him use his leg, and a magnet, to move a needle on the table overhead. At his sittings Slade always wore a pair of loose slippers, out of which he could easily slip. That spectral hand that popped up at the edge of the table? Probably his foot!

Slade even put his *knees* to use—to play the accordion jointly with a spirit. Hereward Carrington, in *The Physical Phenomena of Spiritualism, Fraudulent and Genuine* (1907), tells how it was done:

> The trick is simple enough. In the act of placing the accordion under the table, the medium turned it end for end, so that the end with the keys or notes is now in his hand, and the strap end hanging downward. This lower end the medium grasps between his knees, and, by flexing his wrist strongly, he can play the instrument after a fashion, which is all that is required. Before the accordion is brought up

---

* For more on slate-writing and its various methods, see *Spirit Slate Writing and Kindred Phenomena* (1898) by William E. Robinson. (Robinson was an assistant to Herrmann the Great, and later performed as Chung Ling Soo, a supposedly Chinese conjurer.)

again, the medium is careful to reverse the ends, so that the end containing the notes again hangs downward, as at first.

And his knees had another use. Standing beside a sitter who was not too heavy, Slade could covertly insert his knee beneath the chair and levitate it.

But how did he accomplish that materialization of Alcinda, his late wife? In a dimly-lit room the three women had seen her face, emerging from a swirl of mist. Yet might it not have been a *portrait* of Alcinda, animated by a confederate, that they had seen? Slade is known to have possessed a portrait of her. He had once pointed it out to a visitor, who told a reporter:

> "About three years ago I was introduced to the spirit medium Henry Slade, by a prominent member of the New York bar. A short time afterward I called at the doctor's residence in West Twenty-first street, New York, about eleven o'clock in the morning. I found him smoking a fragrant cigar, and we conversed for some time on the subject of spiritualism. The doctor said it must become a universal belief, and pointing to a large portrait over the mantel he said, 'There is a portrait I painted, while under spirit control, in one hour, and it would take a painter of considerable skill to do it in four days. It is a true picture of my wife, Allie, who passed to spirit life about two years ago. She is now one of my controlling guides, and an Indian named Owasso is another. These guides are always with me.'" (*Brooklyn Daily Eagle*, February 18, 1877)

•

There were Spiritualists, such as Arthur Conan Doyle, who refused to believe that Slade's manifestations had been faked. Doyle pointed to Bellachini's affidavit, attesting to their genuineness. Yet that sworn statement—was *it* genuine? That is to say, how sincere was Bellachini?

It is possible, of course, that he was entirely sincere, but mistaken. Surely even Bellachini could be fooled. Fraudulent mediums were something new on the scene; and magicians were not yet familiar with their techniques. Yet it is hard to believe that a magician would not have recognized one of his own brethren.

Isn't it more likely that Bellachini recognized Slade for what he was—and chose not to expose him? Perhaps he simply wished to help a brother magician earn a living. Or perhaps he enjoyed playing the role of confederate, in someone else's act. Or perhaps he was playing a joke—on those "highly-esteemed gentlemen of rank and position" who had sought his opinion. Or on the scientists, like Zöllner, who were eager to study Slade's "phenomenal" powers. True, Bellachini had signed an affidavit. But does not their profession confer upon conjurers a special dispensation—a license to lie? ("I have here an ordinary deck of cards....")

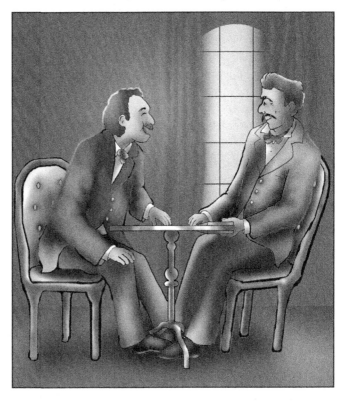

It is a sobering thought that Zöllner cited Slade's powers as evidence for his theory of a fourth dimension. For that theory, while faulty, helped pave the way for the theory of relativity (where *time* is the fourth dimension) and quantum mechanics. Thus, Henry Slade—a fraudulent medium! —played a role in unraveling the mysteries of the universe.

Yet what greater mystery than Slade himself? He began his career as a healer—a "spiritual doctor"—and became a medium. But did he believe in the spirits? Or was it all a humbug from the start? Did he feel any guilt for his false assurances that the soul survived? Or did he justify his trickery on the grounds that there *was* a world beyond, and these communications from its inhabitants, although bogus, were consoling? And where, one wonders, did he acquire his conjuring skills?

One wonders too about his marriage to Alcinda Wilhelm. She was a respected figure among Spiritualists—a well-known physician, lecturer, and reformer. *Had he fooled her too?* Or did she know him for what he was, and—enamoured—not care? (Perhaps she hoped to reform him!)

Alcinda became his spirit guide, along with Owasso and Dr. Davis. Could the spirit of his late wife have been real to Slade? Or was she just part of his act? In any case, when she had materialized that afternoon in front of the three Spiritualists, he had been unnerved:

> My two friends [reports Emma Hardinge] recognised Alcinda Wilhelm as clearly as I did; but Mr. Slade, who seemed very nervous, did not turn his head to look at her until she had gradually melted into the indistinct white mist.

Alcinda had emerged from the mist, gazed at Slade and his guests, and faded away. Spirit or illusion, she was with him yet.

Otto Maurer

OR MANY YEARS A MAGIC SHOP WAS LOCATED AT 321
Bowery, across from the Globe Dime Museum. It was
called Otto Maurer's Magical Bazaar, and occupied
the basement of a five-story tenement. Maurer, the proprietor, lived around the corner, but spent most of his time at
the shop. (Its hours were 6:00 a.m. to 9:00 p.m., including
Sundays.) His customers were both professional and amateur magicians, some of whom performed at the Globe or at
other dime museums on the Bowery. They came to him for
new illusions, or for repairs to the old.

Born in 1846, Maurer had emigrated from Germany as
a young man. In Manhattan he had gone into business as
a tinsmith, fashioning such things as the shades for oil
lamps. But eventually he developed an unusual specialty:
the making of magical apparatus. (In Germany he had
been an amateur magician.) And by the 1880s he was a
leading supplier, shipping apparatus to conjurers around
the country.

Maurer's shop sold both his own creations and those of
others; and his catalogue grew into a 128-page cabinet of
wonders. Profusely illustrated, it advertised such items as
the Inexhaustible Box, the Tea-pot of Mephistopheles, and
the Wonderful Speaking Head. On the cover was a view
(fanciful, as we shall see) of the shop's exterior. On the first
page was a portrait of the proprietor—an eccentric-looking
man, with a prominent forehead, pince-nez glasses, extravagant mustache, and goatee. He was identified as "Otto
Maurer, Professor of Legerdemain." For while primarily a
craftsman, Maurer also performed ("Takes Engagements
for Evening Party & Parlor Entertainments") and gave lessons in sleight of hand. And he was an accomplished performer. According to a review in the *Herald,* "Prof. Otto

Maurer's magical entertainment last evening was the best of the season without doubt."

Henry Ridgely Evans, the historian of magic, once paid a visit to the shop. Years later he would recall his disappointment:

> Maurer, a German-American, kept a little magic emporium on the Bowery. He is dead and gone long ago. His catalogue of tricks was a stupendous affair, with a flamboyant cover, upon which was depicted a splendid show window containing the most gorgeous magical apparatus in the world, displayed for sale. As a callow amateur of nineteen, I made a special pilgrimage from Baltimore to New York to consult Maurer about an outfit I wished to purchase. Up and down the Bowery I walked, looking in vain for the brilliant bazaar of magic and mystery—the number of which I had forgotten to note on the catalogue. Finally, I saw a dirty little gamin playing in the gutter. I questioned him about Maurer. "The feller as sells tricks?" he exclaimed. "Cross the street, Mister, and down them cellar stairs, and you'll find his shop." I fell from Olympus to Hades. Imagine my astonishment to find the Aladdin's palace of enchantment in the cellar of a grimy old tumble-down house. My gorgeous dream was dispelled....His magnificent magical salon was a myth. (*The Old and the New Magic*)

Yet the place was not without an atmosphere of mystery. A reporter from the *World* visited it, and provided this account:

> There is a queer little shop in a Bowery basement where half the jugglers and magicians in the country order their "props." It is presided over by Otto Maurer....If you go down the narrow stairway you will see no one within, but if you wait a few moments a curtain will be drawn, giving you a momentary glimpse of a dimly lighted room beneath the sidewalk, and the magician will appear before

your eyes.

He may not seem particularly overjoyed to meet you, for his habitation is full of dark secrets, and his black art interests him much more than intercourse with his fellow men. What there is in the dark little chamber behind the curtain no one besides himself can tell. He guards its secrets as he does his life. There it is that he conceives the magic devices which line the walls without.

The Bowery magician's den was invaded by a reporter recently. There was apparently not a soul there. The reporter looked around. There was a picture on the wall. He turned suddenly and was startled to find the original of the picture face to face before him. He had not entered by the staircase, and there was evidently no other means of ingress. The dark curtain in the dark little corner only explained the mystery when it was later pointed out by Professor Maurer.

The magician did not have on his performing costume. He was in his shirt sleeves and wore old trousers. His hands were black and grimy, as though he had been working at a forge....

"Let me take your hat," said the professor.

The reporter passed it over. As he did so something tapped him slightly on the top of the head. The reporter looked up, but saw nothing. A slight chill came over him. Was there anything behind him? He turned to look, and caught a glimpse of a skeleton hand as it vanished into air.

Maurer died in January 1900 after an illness. An obituary in the *Herald* was headlined "WIZARD OF THE BOWERY IS DEAD." It described his shop as resembling "an abode of gnomes." And the *Evening Telegraph* lamented that "the Bowery has lost one of its quaintest characters." His son, Otto Maurer, Jr., took over the business. But without its master craftsman, it lasted just three more years.

Today, the Bowery has been gentrified. Yet remnants of its rambunctious past are still to be found. And that abode of gnomes—has any trace of it survived? Is there any relic of Otto Maurer's shop? Curious to find out, one might go today to 321 Bowery; behold the sleek apartment building that has replaced the tenement; and looking downward, wonder what remains of that "dimly lighted room beneath the sidewalk."

The Bangs Sisters

E DWARD AND MEROE BANGS HAD MOVED FROM ATCHI-
son, Kansas, to Chicago in 1861. Edward was a tinsmith and stove repairman; Meroe was a spirit medium.
They had come to Chicago in search of a livelihood in their
respective trades.

The couple had two daughters, Lizzie and May, and two
sons. As soon as the girls were old enough, they were given
a role in the séances, conducted by Meroe in the family
home. Their participation served to allay suspicions of
trickery. A reporter from the *Religio-Philosophical Journal,* a
Spiritualist newspaper, attended a séance, and was charmed
by the girls. In an article titled "An Evening with the Bangs
Children," he extolled their virtues:

> It must be remembered that these mediums are young chil-
> dren. There is not a particle of deception in their nature.
> Their hearts are free from guile, and in all their actions they
> exhibit the innocence of their nature. No one would accuse
> them of deception.

The reality, of course, was that the séances relied heavily
on deception. For Meroe (like most professional mediums)
was essentially a conjurer—one whose purpose, however,
was not to entertain. Rather, it was to dupe, by pretending
to contact the spirit world. Convinced that Meroe was com-
municating with the departed, her clients suffered an additional departure—of their dollars.

As the sisters grew older and more proficient, they took
over the séances, with Meroe serving as their helper. In a
darkened parlor Lizzie or May would enter a trance (or so
it appeared), and summon the spirits. And the spirits came,
writing messages on a slate; blowing on a trumpet; causing

a chair to dance about. May would be tied up inside a cabinet. With her in the cabinet were a guitar and a bell. When the doors were shut, a strumming on the guitar was heard, and a ringing of the bell. May was securely bound (or so it was claimed). So who was doing this? *A spectral hand emerged from an aperture and waved.*

The séances were held in the evening and were open to the public. (During the day, the sisters offered private sittings.) They were advertised in newspapers and cost one dollar to attend. Attendance grew; and the Bangses prospered. On occasion, though, they were harassed by the authorities. In 1881 May and her mother were arrested and charged with keeping a place of amusement without a license. They defended themselves by claiming to be practicing their religion—Spiritualism; and the charges were dropped.

By the end of the decade, dozens of mediums were operating in Chicago. And the police were leaving them alone —unless there was a complaint. In the spring of 1888, a criminal complaint was lodged against the Bangs sisters, the busiest mediums in the city. It came from the *Religio-Philosophical Journal,* which initially had supported their mediumship.

The editor of the *Journal* was Colonel John Bundy. Bundy was both an ardent Spiritualist and the sworn enemy of fake mediums. He deplored their effect on the credibility of Spiritualism, as well as their blatant criminality, and had dedicated himself to exposing them. Once it became evident that the Bangses were frauds, Bundy had resolved to take legal action. But first he had met with the sisters and pleaded with them to desist:

> I desired, as did all who were members of the circle, to save these young women from the disgrace of an exposure, to awaken their moral sense, to portray the danger they were constantly incurring, and to lead them to discontinue their deceptive practices. But pleading and argument proved of no avail. We met, six of us, at the Bangs residence of a

Sunday morning, some weeks ago, and had a two hours' session, during which we exhausted every argument, pointed out some of the deceptions they were guilty of, pleaded with the mother to think of the welfare of her daughters and of the innocent grandchildren who sat in the room with us.

So on April 1, 1888—it was Easter Sunday—Bundy instigated a raid on the Bangses. The raiding party consisted of two plain-clothes policemen, armed with arrest warrants, and several of Bundy's friends. (He himself would have been recognized by the sisters, alerting them to the raid.) In an article titled "The Bangs Sisters Exposed," the *Journal* would describe what transpired:

> On Sunday evening last, while several societies in this city were celebrating the fortieth anniversary of Modern American Spiritualism, and all the churches were filled to overflowing with people who thronged them to hear the beautiful music and witness the floral display, a very different scene was in progress at the home of the Bangs Sisters on Walnut street. While church bells were ringing, organs pealing forth joyful anthems and trained voices filling the air with triumphant strains in commemoration of the resurrection of Jesus, the Bangs women, mother and daughters, were busily engaged in the cold-blooded, damnable, unutterably vile business of running a bogus materialization show. With a music box making noise enough to drown all other sounds and Mrs. Bangs ever on the alert with her cracked voice to fill up any hiatus of the machine music, the daughters went through the sickening swindle with all the coolness of well-trained performers.

The raiding party had entered the parlor, found seats, and—seeking to blend in—joined in the singing of hymns. After a while the lights were dimmed and the séance began. The spirit cabinet was shown to be empty, except for a chair. May got inside and was bound to the chair. The cabinet was divided by a partition into two sections. One was for May; the other for the spirits who were about to materialize. The cabinet doors were shut; and Lizzie, seated beside the cabinet, cranked up the music box.

A curtain opened in the upper half of the spirits' door; and one by one, they began to appear. Barely visible in the dark, they peered out at the attendees. Among them was the spirit of George Bangs. "O that's my brother who died in the war!" cried Lizzie, as the ghostly figure loomed in the opening.

Finally, the main attraction of the evening appeared: the spirit of a Russian princess. She wore a white headdress and a white gown that was spangled with sequins. Seated in the front row, the leader of the raiding party decided it was time.

"There was a signal agreed upon by me and my friends, which I gave when the auspicious moment arrived for making the exposure, and at the same time I made a sudden spring and caught the Princess just before she got the door closed, and I did not release my hold until she was taken before those present, some sixty ladies and gentlemen, with her toggery [outer garment] still upon her, and held by me and my assistants; and when this was torn off of her, the medium, May Bangs, was revealed, dressed the same as she was when she first entered the cabinet. She had in her possession a bundle of paraphernalia, consisting of robes, scarfs, false beards, etc. The mother, fighting to release her, grabbed the bundle, and tried to carry it off, but was intercepted by one of the policemen, who took it from her. The friends of the mediums were so pugnacious that the policemen were compelled to flourish their revolvers in order to maintain order."

A patrol wagon was summoned; and the sisters were taken to the station house. Taken too were the spirit cabinet and the costumes. The *Journal* declined to reveal the workings of the cabinet:

We do not care to give further details of the construction of the trick partition as it would aid those who are following the same diabolical business, but who have not thus far been fortunate enough to secure such a cabinet. They are made however by dealers in conjuring goods and can be bought in any of the larger cities or ordered from Philadelphia, New York and Boston.

Colonel Bundy denounced the sisters. "Their moral obliquity is something shocking. In all my experience I never saw it surpassed and seldom equaled." He also reassured his readers:

Most of you are Spiritualists, and no amount of detected deception can shake your confidence in the evidence you have received of the continuity of life and the facts of intercommunication between the two worlds. You should be strong and heroic, with this faith posited on knowledge.

The Bangs sisters were charged with obtaining money under false pretenses. They denied the accusation, claiming that the theatrical paraphernalia—wigs, costumes, make-up—had been planted by the police. A grand jury listened to the testimony of witnesses. There seemed little doubt as to what the Bangses had been doing in their parlor that evening. But apparently, the jurors deemed the impersonation of spirits to be a permissible activity—a form of theatre, perhaps. For the charges were dismissed.

In June the sisters wrote a letter to the *Tribune,* denouncing the "cowardly raid" on their home. The charges had been baseless, they declared. And they asked the newspaper to publicize the failure of "this effort to degrade and humiliate us."

The Bangs sisters resumed their séances. And they continued to include the materialization of spirits. Only when a law was enacted by the Illinois legislature, in 1891, making it a crime to impersonate the spirits of the dead, did they finally desist.

During their private sittings, the sisters featured the use of slates. A message from the spirit world would mysteriously appear, written on a slate. Or clients were told to bring in a sealed envelope, containing a letter to the departed and blank sheets of paper. The medium placed this envelope between two slates and secured them with rubber bands. At all times the slates remained on the table, in full view—though occasionally half-covered by a tablet. Yet when the envelope was removed, the sheets of paper were found to be filled with writing—a message from the departed.

In this deception too the Bangses were eventually exposed, by Stanley Krebs (who would also expose Henry Slade). During a sitting with May, Krebs secretly positioned a mirror in his lap. And he saw his sealed envelope—supposedly bound between the slates—fall into her lap. Then, reaching down to the floor, May placed the envelope onto a tray with a long handle; and Krebs watched as the tray disappeared under a door. Half an hour later, it re-emerged with his envelope. He was certain that Lizzie—stationed in the next room—had steamed the envelope open, read his letter, and written a response.

And how had May obtained the envelope from between the slates? When she turned her back to Krebs, he seized the opportunity:

> I quickly reached over, carefully picked up the two bound slates and…saw a *small wedge sticking between the slates, thus prising them open wide enough to allow not too fat a letter to slide out through the space thus made between them!*

The wedge had been inserted there, he realized, under cover of the tablet. And picking up the slates at one point, May had allowed the envelope to fall into her lap.

When a second opportunity arose, Krebs peeked between the slates; and indeed, the envelope was gone. Soon thereafter, May retrieved it from the tray. With her sleight-of-hand skills—and under cover of tablets—she *"slipped the letter back into place between the slates,* withdrew the wedge between her fingers under the tablet, removed the tablets, and all was done, in far less time, too, than it takes to tell it."

Krebs himself was nearly exposed, when May caught him glancing downward. Suspicious, and wary of investigators, she asked: "Have you a looking-glass in your lap?" His denial was convincing; and the sitting continued. May would regret having failed to identify Krebs as an investigator. For his detailed exposé appeared in the January 1901 issue of *The Journal of the Society for Psychical Research.* It was titled "A Description of some Trick Methods used by Miss Bangs, of Chicago."

The sisters would occasionally come up with a new trick. In the early nineties they introduced the spirit typewriter. It was placed inside the cabinet; the doors were shut; and a spirit typist tapped out messages—including one from Moses!*

It was around this time that an innovative idea occurred to Lizzie and May. Their spirit friends could be put to work as portrait artists. For if the spirits could write, they could also paint. And in the fall of 1894, the sisters added something truly wondrous to their repertoire: spirit portraits.

Artwork by spirits had been around for a while. Its leading purveyor was a medium known as Madame Diss Debar. She would summon the spirits of artists such as Raphael and Rembrandt; and paintings by them would materialize on blank canvases. Astounded by the materializations, and eager to own the work of a great artist, her clients paid large

---

* A former press agent for the Bangses told a reporter: "When I was traveling with the sisters their typewriter trick was their biggest drawing card. The writing machine was placed in a dark cabinet, where it pounded away for dear life. Presently a typewritten message was slipped out of the cabinet. Every one of these messages is prepared in advance. The typewriter keys are pounded in the cabinet, but what they write there would be unintelligible even to a first-class spook."

sums for these paintings.*

How was it done? Herrmann the Great wrote an exposé for the New York *Herald*. In "How the Spirits Paint in Oils" he explains:

> There are several ways of producing spirit oil paintings. The method of Diss De Bar was as follows:—She would place her dupe in a chair and give him a plain canvas, which he would hold in a horizontal position over his head. She would then take her position behind him, where, of course, it was impossible for him to see any movement she made. Then she would take the painting from underneath her clothing, and by telling him that he was not holding the frame right, take it from his hands for a second and deftly substitute the painted picture.

---

* Madame Diss Debar (one of many aliases used by Anne O'Delia Salomon) was an itinerant swindler who spent time in jail in both the U.S. and Great Britain; established a College of Occult Sciences in South Africa; and ran a fruitarian colony in Florida. In *Beware Familiar Spirits*, John Mulholland calls her "the greatest rogue that ever used spirits to defraud."

One of her incarcerations was for swindling an elderly man, whom she had married for that purpose. Such marriages were a nefarious sideline of some mediums, May Bangs included. May was married four times—twice to elderly men. One of them was Henry Graham, a wealthy manufacturer whose late wife had urged him (via a spirit communication) to marry May. The marriage was short-lived. The other was Jacob Lesher, also a wealthy manufacturer. When he died, after two years of marriage, Lesher was penniless. The *Tribune* reported: "Business tips from the spirits would be blamed for the failure of Jacob Lesher, formerly rated a millionaire, and the husband of May Bangs, a 'spirit painter.'" May undoubtedly profited from both marriages.

Diss Debar was grotesquely fat, and probably weighed as much as both Bangs sisters (described as "good looking...but rather inclined to stoutness") put together.

Herrmann also described a chemical method. The medium coats a painting with a preparation that gives it the appearance of a blank canvas. When later she vigorously rubs the canvas (as instructed by the spirit), this coating evaporates; and the painting emerges.

Lizzie and May set out to materialize paintings, but with a new and lucrative twist. For in their version of the scam, the spirit would create neither a landscape nor a still life. Instead, he would paint a portrait for the client—of a departed loved one.

To achieve this, the sisters initially used a substitution trick similar to that of Diss Debar. They would have a client bring in a photo of the departed. It was sealed in an envelope; and the client was told to return the next day—conditions were not yet favorable. The envelope was then steamed open and the photo conveyed to an artist in their employ. (According to that former press agent, it was a student at the Chicago Art Institute.) Working quickly, the artist painted a portrait.

When the client came back the next day, one of the sisters led him to an upstairs room. There a blank canvas was selected and inspected, then wrapped in paper. As they returned to the parlor, the sister carried the canvas—and made the switch.

The wrapped canvas, supposedly blank, was placed on a table. Summoned from the realm of the dead, the spirit artist went to work on it. And when the wrapping was removed—a portrait of the departed! Thrilled, the client purchased it.

Their business card now advertised "Life Sized Spirit Portraits a Specialty." So popular did this specialty become that the Bangses eventually dropped the public séances, the slate-writing, and the rest. They could charge more than a hundred dollars for a portrait. And clients were more than willing to pay—especially after the sisters devised a way to materialize a portrait *in full view.* The process was called "precipitation"; and by all accounts, was an amazing thing to witness.

It took a spirit about twenty minutes to precipitate a portrait. A pair of framed canvases were shown to be empty. They were stood upright on a small table, face to face, and propped against a window. Sunlight shone through the canvases. A trayful of paints was placed beside them. Seating themselves on either side of the table, the sisters held onto the canvases and summoned the spirit.

And a portrait began to form, as the client watched in awe. Initially, a rosy glow became visible. Then vague patches of color appeared. These resolved themselves into shapes, which became increasingly detailed. One of their clients describes this gradual formation:

> I noticed a pale pink, almost directly in the center. It seemed like the glow of sunrise, but there was no form. Next we noticed an outline. The face was forming. We noticed two dark blurs that grew more distinct, and we saw that they were eyebrows and eyelashes of closed eyes. The lines of the mouth appeared, and the outlines of the head became visible, while the shoulders were distinct; and then the eyes opened out, giving a life-like effect to the portrait.
>
> Was I dreaming? I felt like pinching myself to see. A woman's face was looking at us from between the canvases, beautiful in form and feature.

The canvases were then laid flat on the table and covered —to aid in the setting of the colors, explained the sisters. Finally, the portrait was presented to the client.

The portraits sparked a controversy. Many Spiritualists welcomed them, as gifts from the spirit world and evidence of survival. But Professor Stoller of the Chicago Spiritualist League deemed them to be fraudulent and called for an investigation. Speaking at a meeting of the League, he said:

> There is no such thing as a "spirit painting." Those paintings are the work of human hands. Do you suppose a spirit is going to return to this earth with its sin, corruption, crime, and commercialism to paint pictures for the pecuniary gain of some medium? I think not. Spirits are not

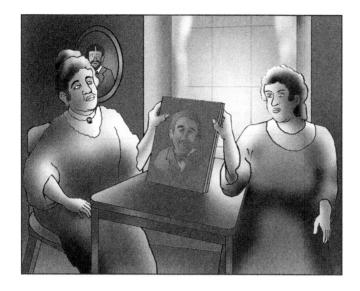

actuated by such mercenary motives. It is the mediums who are after the money, not the spirits. I should hate to think of any self-respecting spirit doing such things.

But it was a convincing illusion—one that astonished all who saw it. The precipitations defied explanation. Not even magicians could figure out how it was done. And despite the accusations of fraud, Lizzie and May continued to attract clients, materialize portraits, and take in dollars. "We are the only people in the world today," May insisted, "who positively and absolutely prove immortality."

One magician, however, was determined to learn the secret. David Abbott was the author of *Behind the Scenes with the Mediums* (1907), an exposé of mediumistic deceptions. Yet the spirit portraits had him baffled. And welcoming the challenge, he resolved to figure out how the paintings were produced.

Almost by accident, he succeeded in doing so. In a 1913 article, "The Spirit Portrait Mystery: Its Final Solution," Abbott recounts his discovery of the secret:

It is now about four years since I made a discovery that finally cleared up one of the greatest of mediumistic mysteries. For about fifteen years the feat of producing spirit portraits has baffled all of the investigators that have studied the problem. Through its agency some of our most prominent men have been converted to spiritualism, and conjurers have universally acknowledged it to be the most miraculous phenomenon that ever confronted them. Meanwhile two famous lady mediums of Chicago have continued to produce these wonderful portraits as the work of the spirit world.

Abbott had begun with a basic assumption: no spirit was involved in the creation of a spirit portrait. Obviously, it was a conjurer's effect, based on some new and ingenious principle. He reviewed various theories: there was a removable layer of canvas over the portrait; or a chemical coating that was wiped away; or a secret panel in the window. But none of these could explain precipitation—the *gradual* appearance of the portrait.

Both canvases had been examined and verified to be blank. So at some point a substitution must have been made. Employing misdirection and sleight of hand, the sisters could easily have substituted a painted canvas for one of the blank ones. The mystery was the precipitation. How had a gradual materialization—in full view of the client—been effected? And why, Abbott wondered, had two canvases been necessary?

He constructed a model. It consisted of two translucent canvases, opposite one another. One of them was blank; the other had a portrait painted on it. Abbott placed his model in front of a window, allowing sunlight to shine through it. And he began to experiment. He had heard rumors that a graduated screen—a roll of gauze that became increasingly less opaque—was secretly placed between the canvases. What would be the effect of such a screen?

To find out, Abbott mounted a pair of rollers on a frame, and installed on them a length of graduated gauze. He placed this screen between the blank canvas and the portrait, and began to wind it along. As the gauze became less opaque, shadowy patches became visible.

These results, though promising, were inconclusive. But when he removed the screen and brought the canvases together—touching one another—something remarkable occurred:

The portrait, viewed from the front through the blank canvas, immediately became clear and sharp. I again moved the portrait backward, viewing it through the front one. It grew indistinct, more and more "out of focus," until it became an indistinct cloud, then merely some dim shadows; and finally it vanished utterly leaving the canvas clear and white. I brought it forward slowly, and it gradually made its appearance, the dark lines first appearing, then the rosy glow at the center; and finally the features began to form; and at last the eyes changed from dark shadowy rings, to open, bright eyes.

I looked on in awe. Here was the very thing for which I was searching, and without screen of graduated gauze, or apparatus. Here was the long-sought subtle principle, the famous secret that had baffled scientists and the investigators of the world; and it was a thing so simple that it staggered me.

The sisters had utilized a simple principle of optics. And Abbott came up with the following scenario for their precipitation of a spirit portrait:

The Bangses began (like the conjurers that they were) by allowing the client to select, and thoroughly examine, two blank canvases. Meanwhile, the portrait—prepared in advance from a photograph—was close at hand. Perhaps it was hidden behind the drapery of the window, or under the skirt of one of the sisters. (Abbott suspected the skirt: "I have always found that female mediums do not hesitate to take advantage of their sex and the sacredness of their skirts, to cover deception.") One sister then distracted the client, while the other made the substitution. Thus, only one of the canvases placed before the window was blank. The other, in the rear, was the portrait—ready to be precipitated.

> The sitter naturally thinks that his two chosen blanks are now in the window, and he seems to be seeing right through them and they appear clear and white. He does not dream that his portrait, all finished, is already in the window behind the front canvas, but merely moved back out of focus.

Lizzie and May sat beside the table and held onto the canvases. Ostensibly, this was to steady them, and to facilitate the flow of energy from the spirit world. Actually, the sisters were about to manipulate the portrait.

The canvases were several inches apart—far enough to allow the sunlight, as it passed through the portrait in the rear, to diffuse and scatter. Thus, both canvases appeared to be clear and white. Slowly, the sisters moved the portrait forward. And gradually, like an image coming into focus, the portrait became visible. It was seen *through* the translucent canvas in front of it. Patches of color, then vague outlines, then facial features. And finally, as the canvases touched, the finished portrait.

The sisters laid the canvases flat and covered them—supposedly to help set the colors. Actually, this was to hide a sleight-of-hand move that left the portrait uppermost. They then uncovered the portrait and handed it to the client. To complete the illusion, they had applied to it earlier a greasy substance; and the portrait seemed freshly painted.

Such was Abbott's solution to the mystery. He told a fellow magician, Dr. Wilmar, about it. Wilmar perfected the method; designed a stage illusion based on it; and sold the rights to a British performer named Selbert. In 1910 Selbert toured with a spirit painting act. And the following year Howard Thurston added the illusion to his show. Thurston had the audience select a famous person to be depicted. His poster (advertising "Abbott's Riddle of the Century,

World's Celebrities Painted by Spirit Hands") showed him materializing a portrait of Napoleon. And two mentalists, Dunninger and Alexander, did spirit paintings. Alexander added a commercial touch. His paintings contained ads for local businesses.

The spirits had migrated from the séance room to the vaudeville stage. But some of them had stayed behind. For the Bangs sisters were still summoning spirit artists and commissioning portraits. Despite the competition from magicians, the sisters remained in business.

They continued to practice their deceptions and take in dollars. They also continued to avoid prosecution. During a life-long career of criminal fraud, the Bangs sisters spent only a single night in jail. That was on Easter Sunday in 1888, after the raid by Colonel Bundy's party. On that Sunday May Bangs had impersonated spirits, as church bells rang throughout the city—in celebration of an actual return from the dead.

Servais Le Roy

S ERVAIS LE ROY WAS BORN IN SPA, BELGIUM, IN 1865, the son of a Belgian hotel manager and a British mother. When he was twelve, he ran away from home and wound up in England. A family there took him in and raised him.

The family had a magician friend, whose tricks fascinated Le Roy and inspired him to study magic. He became proficient in the art. And by the age of 21, he was performing professionally.

His first major booking was at the Royal Aquarium. While there, he met Mary Ann Ford, who was assisting a mindreader. She became Le Roy's assistant and, soon thereafter, his wife. As "Talma," she would become an integral part of his act.

During the nineteenth century, magicians were notorious for copying the illusions of others. But Servais Le Roy never copied. All of his illusions were original—the product of his inventiveness, technical skills, and artistry. His earliest was called The Three Graces. A cabinet was shown to be empty. Le Roy spun the open cabinet around, to show all of its sides. Then he held a large cloth in front of it. And one by one, he produced the Three Graces out of the cabinet.

Whence these goddesses? They had been inside the cabinet all along, of course—concealed behind a pair of mirrors. The mirrors were angled to reflect the interior walls, thus creating the illusion of an empty cabinet.

The Three Graces was such a success that Le Roy took it on tour. He and Talma sailed to America, where they performed in Boston and other cities. A year later they were back in England, working on his next creation: The Flying Visit.

The Flying Visit premiered at the London Palladium. The curtain rose to reveal a pair of cabinets. One, with short legs, was on the floor of the stage. The other, a distance away and mounted on stilts, was accessible only by a ladder. Each cabinet had a curtained front. The curtains were open, to reveal the interiors.

Le Roy came on stage, wearing a red skullcap, pointed beard, and harlequin-style suit. He was costumed as Mephistopheles. With a courtly bow, he addressed the audience. They could see that the cabinets were empty, he said. Moreover, both cabinets were raised from the floor, which precluded the use of a trapdoor. He sauntered about the stage, as if inspecting it. Then, with a wave, he climbed into the lower cabinet and closed the curtain behind him.

Almost immediately, the curtain reopened—to reveal Talma. The magician was gone and had been replaced by his assistant. Jumping out of the cabinet, she cried: "Where are you?"

"I am here!"

The reply had come from the other cabinet, high above the stage. Peering out of it, like a boy in a tree-house, was Le Roy. He ducked back inside and closed the curtain.

Talma rushed over, climbed the ladder, and flung open the curtain. To her dismay, the cabinet was empty. "Where are you now?" she called out.

"I am here!" came a shout from the rear of the theatre. It was Le Roy. A spotlight followed him as he ran down the aisle. Talma climbed back down. Le Roy bounded onto the stage and took her hand. And together they acknowledged the applause.

How was it done? How had Mephistopheles flown invisibly from one cabinet to the other, and then to the rear of the theatre? What devilry was afoot here?

The secret was simple yet ingenious. To the magician's bag of tricks, Le Roy had added something new: a practice that became known as "doubling." Two male assistants were involved. Of the same build as Le Roy, they had donned costumes identical to his. Thus, *three* Mephistopheles took part in the illusion. And from a distance, they were indistinguishable from one another.

While sauntering about the stage, Le Roy had stepped behind a side-scene—*and one of the doubles had stepped out, taking his place.* The switch was well-rehearsed, perfectly timed, and undetectable, like a sleight-of-hand move. Thus, it was the double who had climbed into the cabinet. And drawing the curtain, he had switched places with Talma, who had been concealed behind a mirror.

And it was the second double, concealed in the upper cabinet, who had peered out and cried: "I am here!" Drawing the curtain, he returned to his hiding place. And Talma, climbing the ladder, found the cabinet to be (seemingly) empty.

Meanwhile, Le Roy (the real one) was racing through the basement of the theatre. There was not a second to spare. Dashing up a stairway, he emerged in the rear of the theatre —just as Talma called out: "Where are you now?" He shouted his reply; and basking in the spotlight, came running down the aisle.

The Flying Visit was a hit in London. And once again they took their act to America. While performing there, Le Roy received a proposal from M. B. Levitt, the theatrical manager. Would he be interested in forming a partnership with two other magicians? Le Roy signed on. And he, Frederick Eugene Powell, and Imre Fox (a comic magician) —the Triple Alliance, as they were called—were booked now as a single, full-evening show. In addition, Le Roy was still performing solo, as a vaudeville act.

Talma too was performing solo. She had shown an aptitude for sleight of hand—in particular, for the manipulation of coins; and Le Roy had been coaching her. Finally, in 1899, "Talma the Queen of Coins" made her debut in a London music hall. (T. Nelson Downs, billed as "the King of Koins," was appearing in London at the same time.) More bookings followed. When not assisting Le Roy, Talma would don a black gown, stick a red rose in her hair, and— often with top billing—perform at variety theatres.

The Triple Alliance eventually broke up. But Le Roy liked the idea of a trio of magicians. So he formed another one. This new partnership would last more than twenty years and achieve international renown. It was called Le Roy, Talma, and Bosco.

Leon Bosco was an acrobat who had grown too heavy for acrobatics. So he re-created himself as a knockabout comedian. His role in the troupe was that of a bumbling magician. Le Roy performed the large-scale illusions; Talma did coin tricks; and Bosco—fat, bald, and bumbling—provided comic relief. The three were billed as the "Comedians de Mephisto." One of their posters shows Le Roy and Talma performing The Flying Visit, as Bosco watches in amazement. Another shows Bosco stuck in a tub, from which the others are trying to extricate him.

Le Roy continued to design and present new illusions. (He also manufactured them for other magicians.) The most celebrated was Asrah the Floating Princess, first performed in London in 1914. Talma was hypnotized, laid out on a table, covered with a sheet, and levitated. A hoop was passed around her, to show that there were no supports. Then the sheet was whipped away—and she was gone! It was a startling illusion—one that is still being performed today.

Among his other illusions were The Vanishing Lion (a lion disappears from its cage, as Talma is flung inside); The Flying Piano (Talma and a piano are levitated); and The Duck Tub (Le Roy and Bosco build a tub and fill it with water; a pistol is fired; and ducks are suddenly swimming in the tub). And in a variation on The Flying Visit, Le Roy vanishes from a cabinet. Then, down in the pit, the orchestra leader turns to face the audience—and it is Le Roy.

In 1913 Leon Bosco was forced to retire, on account of ill health; and he was replaced with a new Bosco. Dr. James William Elliott assumed both the role and the name. Elliott was a physician and amateur magician, who gave up medicine to join the troupe. In order to pass as Bosco, he shaved his head, trimmed his beard, and stuffed a pillow into his vest. And when he too retired, in 1917, yet another Bosco was recruited. Altogether, there were nine Boscos.

The trio performed throughout the 1920s, traveling by

train from engagement to engagement and staying in hotels. But Le Roy and Talma had bought a house in Keansburg, New Jersey. Keansburg was a seaside resort, across the bay from New York. With its amusement park and boardwalk, the town was a congenial place for a pair of vaudevillians.

In 1930, while walking home, Le Roy was struck by a car. He eventually recovered. But though continuing to design and build illusions, he no longer performed. He and Talma retired to a quiet life in Keansburg.

Then, in the summer of 1940, Le Roy returned to the

stage. The Society of American Magicians featured him in a show at the Heckscher Theatre in New York. Meant to honor him, it proved to be a humiliating disaster. There had been only a single rehearsal. Inexperienced assistants brought out the wrong props. And as he performed, Le Roy's fingers trembled. He dropped things, was forgetful, and appeared ill at ease. During the intermission people left the theatre. It was a grim evening for everyone.

Milbourne Christopher, in *The Illustrated History of Magic* (1973), describes its effect on Le Roy:

> The next day—utterly dejected—Le Roy began destroying his tricks, illusions, and the mementos of a long and rewarding career. Until then, he had been working on a book about his adventures and original creations. He never touched his manuscript again after the sad night at the Heckscher.

In 1944 Talma died. They had been together for more than fifty years. Le Roy remained in the Keansburg house, cared for by Talma's sister (who had been a member of the troupe) He died in 1953, at the age of 88.

In his final moments, Le Roy perhaps heard a familiar voice—a cry of "Where are you?" And calling out "I am here!" he raced down an aisle—out of this illusory world and into her arms.

Bert Reese

I N FEBRUARY 1915, BERT REESE WAS ARRESTED AT HIS APART-
ment and charged with fortunetelling, a misdemeanor
in New York City. He was found guilty and given a form
of probation. But Reese, claiming to be an "entertainer" and
not a fortuneteller, appealed the conviction.

The outcome of his appeal was reported in the *Times*:

MIND READER WINS BY FEATS IN COURT

W. Bert Reese, whose "mind reading" demonstrations have
mystified many scientists, including Thomas A. Edison
and Dr. William Hanna Thompson, author of "Brain and
Personality," was discharged yesterday by Judge Rosalsky
in General Sessions on his appeal from a conviction by
Magistrate Barlow of disorderly conduct, under a section
dealing with fortune telling. Reese convinced Judge Rosalsky, Assistant District Attorneys Bostwick and Flint and
two reporters by demonstrations in court that he was not
a disorderly person, but a man with apparently unusual
powers.

Reese was arrested at 230 West Ninety-ninth Street on
Feb. 26 on complaint of Detective Adele Priess, who said
she had paid him $5 to have her fortune told. Reese denied
that he had told her fortune or accepted any money. He was
found guilty and held in $1,000 bonds to keep the peace for
one year.

When his case came before Judge Rosalsky yesterday on
appeal, Reese asked permission to demonstrate his abilities
to the court. He told Judge Rosalsky to write something on
each of three pieces of paper, and to fold them so that he
might not be able to read what had been written. Judge
Rosalsky put the papers in different pockets after he had
mixed them up so that he could not distinguish them

himself. Then Judge Rosalsky produced one of the folded papers and pressed it against Reese's forehead.

"You ask me how much money you have in a certain bank," Reese said. "Fifteen dollars is the answer."

Judge Rosalsky admitted that the answer was correct, and produced the second piece of paper.

"This piece contains the name of one of your old school teachers—Miss O'Connor," Reese said.

The third question, which he read correctly but did not answer, was: "What was the rule in Shelley's case?"

Reese performed similar demonstrations for the benefit of Mr. Bostwick, Mr. Flint, and the reporters. His last feat was to give the maiden name of the mother of one of the reporters. All of the questions were written on General Sessions stationery, which Judge Rosalsky supplied.

"I do not consider you a disorderly person," Judge Rosalsky said, when the demonstrations were finished. "You are honorably discharged."

Reese, who is more than 70 years old, said he had appeared before several of the crowned heads of Europe. It was not his fault, he said, if he had abnormal powers.

Whether Judge Rosalsky credited him with such powers, or simply deemed his prosecution to be absurd, is not known. What is known is that Bert Reese was the most accomplished "billet reader" in the annals of conjuring.

A billet is a slip of paper that has been folded securely or sealed in an envelope; yet the conjurer is able to read what is written on it. Two of the most skillful practitioners of the art, says Theodore Annemann in *Practical Mental Magic*, were Dr. Lynn and the medium Charles Foster. "But in the past 30 years one man stood out as a charlatan par excellence at the business of reading the folded slip. The man was Berthold Riess, born in 1841 in Posen, which was then in Prussia. Later he became known universally as Bert Reese."

Charles Foster—the medium who taught Reese the art —featured billet reading in his séances. Sitters would take a slip of paper, write the name of a departed relative, and roll up the slip. Foster held it to his forehead. With his psychic powers, he was able to read the name—and summon the departed! He would then relay messages from this visiting spirit.

Reese likewise read billets, to demonstrate his psychic powers and gain the confidence of a client. But unlike Foster, he summoned no spirits. Instead, he offered a miscellany of services. He predicted the future, attracted good luck, offered financial tips, etc. Reese claimed to be clairvoyant. In fact, he was a con man, skilled in sleight of hand and psychology. For these were the basic skills of a billet reader.

Little is known of Reese's early years. He immigrated to the U.S. in 1861 and resided initially in New York. There, apparently, he became friendly with Foster, who tutored him in billet reading. Countless hours of practice must have followed, as he learned to manipulate the slips. Finally, he embarked upon a career as a psychic. Perhaps he traveled with a carnival, or plied his trade in taverns.

But eventually, he hung out a shingle. In November 1893, this ad appeared in the Rochester *Democrat and Chronicle*, in the classified section under "Clairvoyants":

> THE GREATEST medium of the age, Professor Bert Reese, 22 North Clinton st., will tell you everything you want to know and guarantee satisfaction or no pay; he has no equal in charm working, his system is with the seven books of Moses, names given in full, sittings two dollars.

Also advertising was "Madam La Rue, celebrated life reader and phrenologist." Both were offering their services to the residents of Rochester.

Yet Reese seems to have moved about. On June 23, 1894, the *Times* published this report from a correspondent in Boston:

> One Prof. Bert Reese, so self-styled, has been in Boston recently, but when looked for by the police today could not

be found. Reese came here three weeks ago and advertised himself as a clairvoyant, claiming to have letters from the highest officials in Chicago addressed to the Chief of Police of Boston....Reese was advised by the police to leave town and he lost no time in going.

In 1894 he was still a small-time psychic, telling fortunes, working charms, and dodging the police. His clientele, like that of Madam La Rue, were the needy, the desperate, the superstitious. But that was about to change. For late in life— he was nearing sixty—Reese set his sights on larger game.

In the summer of 1898, "Professor and Mrs. Bert Reese" were among those listed as new arrivals at the Hotel Savoy in New York. And on September 25, the *Telegraph* published this account:

Those members of the Democratic Club who were around the temporary club rooms in the Hotel Savoy on Friday night were favored with a unique impromptu entertainment, the principal figure in the same being "Prof." Bert Reese, a past master in the art of telepathy or thought transmission. The "Prof.," who comes here from Chicago, although he is originally a German, is an oracle of high ability, and there isn't anything within the bounds of reason that he cannot tell about....the "Prof." has yet to meet the man whose mind he cannot read. He can tell you to a dot how much money you have in your clothes, or any place else for that matter; tell you where you were born naming date and place; tell you where you made your first dollar and who paid it to you, or, in fact, by his simple method of thought transmission, can tell anything that happened in your past life.

The "Prof." has been around New York now for several months, spending his evenings at Shanley's [a popular restaurant], where he has mystified all the habitues and proprietors. He told "Tom" Shanley on one evening to a cent how much cash there was in his drawer, and also how much he had taken in for a certain specified time. In order to believe his feats it is necessary to experience them your-self, as the average mortal would not believe what he had accomplished even if stated under oath.

The article goes on to name the prominent Democrats who were present that night. And it describes what they witnessed:

The "Prof." gave his seance in Parlor D of the hotel. All the members sat around the table and he called on them for questions to answer. Commissioner Cosby asked him to tell his mother's maiden name, and from whom he received his first $100 check; John McDonald asked him the name of the first place he worked and how much money he had in his pocket; Col. Keogh asked him to tell where he had bought his eyeglasses and how much he had paid for them, and the date and place of his birth. *The "Professor" handed around small slips of paper on which the questioners were to write their answers for verification purposes, when he left the room.* [emphasis added] He went out and the questioners did as requested. When he returned the slips of paper, care-fully folded, were handed to Mr. Wallace, the most skepti-cal man in the crowd. He was told to distribute the slips among the group. He did so and the "Professor" answered every one of them correctly, telling just who had each par-ticular question and the answer as he went along.

Reese had sought out these influential men, astonished them, and thus made their acquaintance. During the next twenty years, he would profit from having done so. As word spread of his psychic abilities, the well-to-do sought him out for "consultations." For a hefty fee he would give them both financial and personal advice. He offered tips on stocks, guidance in business affairs, advice on where to drill for oil; and frequently he guessed right. A consultation with Professor Reese became the thing to do. And his own coffers began to fill.

His skill at billet reading was the key to this success; for the readings convinced people that Reese was psychic. What other explanation was there? (Even scientists who tested him were fooled.) But he also had a winning personality—one that charmed his clients. In *Houdini and Conan Doyle: The Story of a Strange Friendship* (1932), Bernard Ernst (a magician) and Hereward Carrington (a psychic researcher) offer this appraisal of Reese:

> Reese was a remarkable character. He was a short, fat, completely bald, well-paunched, cherubic-faced little Polish Jew, with a kindly heart, keen mind and delightful sense of humor. He reminded one of a little gnome, with his pop-eyes and pot-belly. But he was a remarkable personality. He had travelled extensively, and come into contact with royalty and celebrities in many different countries. His home was filled with presents which these individuals had given him. In his tie was a huge diamond pin, which had been given him by the late King of Spain; upon his finger an even bigger diamond presented by the Sovereign of another country. In the opinion of many, Reese possessed remarkable powers—though he certainly added to these, whenever possible, by any normal means possible, and his truly extraordinary insight into human nature and human motives. Thomas Edison, the late Dr. William Hanna Thomson, and many others, publicly affirmed their belief in his preternatural faculties over their own signatures, in the New York *Times*.

That testimonial from Edison was a coup for Reese. The two men had been brought together by Henry Ford. "This man Reese does some strange things," Ford had told the inventor. "I want you to meet him. Perhaps you can explain his power." In 1910 a meeting took place at Edison's laboratory, during which Reese demonstrated his psychic powers. Amazed at what he saw (or thought he saw), Edison concluded that such powers were real; that Reese possessed them; and that a historic moment was at hand. "I believe that this man proves that we are on the verge of new and great discoveries. Some vast new knowledge may well come from Reese, or some such men as Reese, if there are any other men like him."

Persuaded by Reese's feats that mindreading was real, Edison sought to build a device that could induce it. In his diary he recorded the results:

> I tried to solve the phenomena by means of electrical appliances or coils clasped or harnessed about the head. Four of us gathered at one time in four different rooms, each wearing the apparatus adjusted around our heads and all trying to get results. Then we sat in the four corners of the same room, gradually drawing our chairs closer to the center of the room until our knees touched, and still we achieved no results in mindreading.
>
> But Reese needs no apparatus for the demonstration of this peculiar power, and no conditions. He does not reveal his method, if he has any, but has promised me his view of it in his last will and testament.

Reese did indeed have a method for reading minds—one that was simple yet effective. It was comprised of the "billet switch," misdirection, and sheer audacity.

The billet switch was his basic move; and he was a master

of it. Hidden in his hand (or "palmed") was a blank slip, folded to resemble the one that had writing on it. Deftly, by sleight of hand, he would switch the slips. This substitution was made at some opportune moment. If a slip was being held to his forehead, Reese might say, "No, like this." He would take the slip from the subject, show him how to hold it, and hand it back. Or rather, hand back the substitute; for the switch had been made. If there were multiple slips in a pile to be read, he might casually straighten the pile— and while doing so, make the switch. (He only needed to peek at one of them; the contents of the other slips would be learned by the one-ahead method.) Or he might pick up a slip and place it in the subject's pocket—making the switch then. All these moves were virtually invisible, and accompanied by misdirection.

Once he had possession of a slip, Reese was an expert at surreptitiously reading it. (And he used a type of soft paper, to prevent a crinkling sound as he unfolded the slip.) With the slip hidden in his palm, he might rub his forehead—as if concentrating—and sneak a peek. Or he would make use of his cigar. Reese always smoked a cigar during his readings —for its utility. It kept going out; and relighting it provided an opportunity to read the slip. Charles Foster, his mentor, had smoked a cigar for that very purpose.

Reese pretended to read minds. But the thoughts always had to be written down first (supposedly to focus the mind, or for verification)—a condition that should have roused suspicion. John Mulholland, the magic historian, explains:

> When a person, who professes to be a mind-reader, demands that the thoughts to be disclosed must be written, he is a reader of script, in all likelihood, rather than a reader of thoughts....May it suffice to say that there are hundreds of methods used to discover what may be written on a piece of paper....Once you have written something on a piece of paper you may believe with complete confidence that the mind-reader can, if he wishes, read your writing without your knowledge. (*Beware Familiar Spirits*, 1938)

Often, Reese's subjects would swear that he never touched, or even came near, the slips of paper. But they had been misled, says Mulholland:

> Every one whom I have known who understood the methods and psychology of mystification, and who had seen Reese's demonstrations, agreed that he was not only slick manipulatively but that he was extraordinarily clever in misleading and confusing his subjects regarding what really happened.

He *always* touched the slips, and managed to read them. And he always succeeded in deceiving the subject—or almost always. For at least twice in his career Reese was detected and threatened with exposure. It happened once while he was still in Chicago. Joe Rinn, a member of the Society for Psychical Research, had been told by a colleague that Reese was "a real psychic." Skeptical, Rinn made an appointment and came in for a sitting. By secretly numbering his slips, he caught Reese doing the one-ahead trick (in which a psychic pretends to be verifying the contents of a slip, while in fact perusing the contents of the next slip). Reese confessed to fakery, but pleaded with Rinn not to expose him. He was an old man, he said, with no other means of earning a living. Rinn agreed not to expose him, if Reese would present himself as an entertainer and not as a medium.

"Thank you, Mr. Rinn," said Reese. "I promise never to pose as being in contact with the spirit world. I'll allow my clients to figure out for themselves the basis of my powers."

And twenty years later, an equally skeptical Houdini came in for a sitting. In a letter to Arthur Conan Doyle, he describes the encounter:

> A man in New York, named, or calling himself—Dr. Reese, is, without doubt, the cleverest reader of Messages that ever lived.
>
> He has deceived the great minds of Germany—in the Courts—winning a lawsuit, and in America, I know he has

made children of our brainiest men....

Reese knew who I was, when I called for a sitting, and I will say that, of all the clever sleight-of-hand men, he is the brainiest that I have ever come across....

I caught him red-handed, and he acknowledged it was the first time in his life that anyone had ever "recognized his Powers." And I'll put it in writing he was the slickest I have ever seen.

Houdini was conducting a crusade to expose fake mediums and psychics. But when Reese insisted that he was only an entertainer, Houdini relented and left him alone.*

Four years later, however, Houdini was speaking on a New York radio station about fraudulent mediums—and he mentioned billet readers. If they claimed to have abnormal powers, he warned, these men too were frauds. That night Houdini received an irate phone call from Mrs. Reese. When she put her husband on the phone, he angrily denied the accusation of fraud.

The next day Houdini sent Reese a registered letter, containing a challenge. He offered to conduct a test of Reese's abilities, in front of witnesses and with a cash prize. Houdini would have the right to provide the paper for the slips; and Reese would not be permitted to touch them.

> I claim that I can prove that you resort to adroit conjuring and if you can prove to the contrary I will be the first one to shake your hand and acknowledge that you do possess the power attributed to you by the scientists whom you have baffled....I sincerely hope that you will win my money, for, if you do, I will have seen the first case of psychometric clairvoyance in my life, and would gladly pay $1000.

---

* Houdini saved the slips from his sitting (one of which he had folded in a recognizable way) in an envelope on which he wrote "Pellets [billets] size and shape with which I got Dr. Bert Reese." This memento, with its note of triumph, is now in the possession of George Goebel, a Baltimore magician with an extensive knowledge of magic history.

Reese did meet with Houdini. "He came to see me," Houdini would recall, "and begged me not to expose his work, that he was an old man, 83 years of age, and made a living by giving people the idea that he possessed abnormal powers."

A friendly conversation ensued. Houdini asked if he had known Charles Foster. "Yes, I worked with him," said Reese. "He was a good man but he couldn't work for scientists. He wasn't clever enough. I have fooled lots of scientists. I have also advised a great many persons."

Finally, Reese promised to refrain from making claims of mediumship or telepathy. The two conjurers shook hands and parted.

Reese died two years later, in Hamburg. Beset with health problems, he had returned to Germany to visit a spa.

A week after his death, the *Evening Graphic* published an article exposing Reese's methods. Thomas Edison responded:

Dear Sir:

In the Graphic Magazine of Saturday, July 17, 1926, you printed an article by one Samri Frikell in which he claims to "expose" the late Professor W. Bert Reese as a fake medium.

I am certain that Reese was neither a medium nor a fake. I saw him several times and on each occasion I wrote something on a piece of paper when Reese was not near or when he was in another room. In no single case was one of these papers handled by Reese, and some of them he never even saw, yet he recited correctly the contents of each paper.

Several people in my laboratory had the same kind of experience, and there are hundreds of prominent people in New York who can testify to the same thing.

Yours truly,

Thos. A. Edison

Edison gave us the light bulb, that we might better see what was in front of us. Yet he failed to recognize that a conjurer's hand is quicker than the eye.

Charles Morritt

CHARLES MORRITT (1861–1936) WAS THE SON OF A gentleman farmer in the north of England. As a seventeen-year-old he was drawn to conjuring. Years later he would recall his beginnings as a performer:

> Mystery Entertainments first drew my attention in 1877, when a great sensation was caused in England by the Davenport Brothers. The papers gave a description of their amusing performance and the subject so fascinated me that I at once began to study it. The first result was that I made a light wooden seance cabinet, inside which I placed a person, closed the door, and then showed the cabinet empty....
>
> I then set to work to get together a programme of Mysteries with a view to giving my first show. This debut was duly made in 1878, and I may say I had the courage, or audacity, to make my first a full two hours' entertainment at the Public Hall, Selby, Yorks, with no other person on the bill. I advertised extensively and my programme consisted, first, of catching half-crowns in the air and throwing in to a tall hat; then going amongst the audience and taking them from people's noses of the audience, and finally producing a rabbit from a hat. My second item was a series of card tricks, concluding with the rising cards from a bottle, which made a good impression.... My concluding item was "Thought Reading."

By 1880 he was not only performing, but managing several theatres in Leeds. But the young man was ambitious; and eventually he moved on to London. By then he had acquired an assistant: his "sister Lillian," as she was billed. In reality, the two were not siblings, but lovers. On stages in London they performed a mindreading act. It proved popular with audiences; made a name for Morritt; and baffled even magicians.

Mindreading acts often rely on a memorized list, like the one used by Robert Heller. Either the magician or his assistant is blindfolded on stage; and the other circulates among the audience, selecting objects—a hat, a purse, an umbrella —and asking the mindreader to name them. Which he or she does! The secret (as explained in the chapter on Heller) is simple. Both the magician and his assistant have memorized a list. It is comprised of common objects, each linked to a different question—"What am I holding up?" "Can you tell me what this is?" etc. Thus, the question serves to identify the object. No mindreading is required.

Morritt and Lillian used a memorized list—but with an ingenious innovation. No questions were asked. Indeed, Morritt, who did the circulating, said little as he held up objects. But Lillian, blindfolded on the stage, was able to identify them. The secret of the trick? *Synchronized counting.*

Say, for example, that he was holding up an umbrella, and "umbrella" was number 35 on their list. Morritt gave a cue (any sound would do); and he and Lillian began to count, silently to themselves—at *precisely* the same speed. Upon reaching three, Morritt gave another cue; and they began a new count. At five he gave a final cue. Thus was the number 35 communicated to her. This method took precision; but Morritt and Lillian were practiced and in perfect sync. And in a way, it *was* mindreading, so attuned were they to one another.

The popularity of their mindreading act led to further engagements. For nine months they performed in America, on the same bill as Herrmann the Great. Tall, handsome, and clad in evening dress, Morritt brought a winsome elegance to the stage. Returning to London, he was hired by John Nevil Maskelyne; and for three years, was a member of Maskelyne's company, performing at the Egyptian Hall. His repertoire now included sleight of hand, hypnotism, hand-shadows, and large-scale illusions.

But in 1892, craving independence, he left the company to perform on his own—initially at the Empire Theatre, then at Princes' Hall. He was now in competition with his former employer. A review appeared in *The Saturday Review of Politics, Literature, Science, and Art*:

> Mr. Charles Morritt's entertainment, which takes place at Princes' Hall, Piccadilly, every afternoon, is a very varied one, and, by avoiding monotony, he makes it a very attractive one. Mr. Morritt is well known for his sleight of hand, which he has often displayed at the Egyptian Hall, and which is the first proof which he gives in his own entertainment of his powers of conjuring. The Shadowgraphs are also too well known to want further remark here. His cage mystery "Flyto" is ingenious, but his "latest unfathomable mystery, the Missing Lady," is the most seemingly wonderful piece of deception of all. The lady is placed in a chair, is bound round with ropes, hauled up several feet from the ground by a sort of crane in full view of the audience with no curtain near her. Mr. Morritt fires a pistol and she is gone in one second, the empty chair remaining!*

And a review in *Pick-me-up* was equally favorable:

> Mr. Morritt's faculty for bringing cards from anywhere is quite remarkable. He got some poor fellow on the stage, and fished about two packs out of his shirt front for a start; and then he brought a pack or two more from his victim's nose in the most ludicrous manner possible. Later on in the evening Mr. Morritt showed us some clever "shadowgraph" pictures which he made on a screen with his hands, some of the effects produced being really wonderful.

---

* Also on the bill at Princes' Hall were a musical dog and a banjo player. Morritt's act was popular; but when ticket sales began to decline, he replaced the lady in the chair with the Tichborne Claimant. A notorious figure, the Tichborne Claimant was a butcher who had falsely claimed to be the heir to a family fortune. Convicted of fraud, he was imprisoned; and after his release, Morritt hired him to vanish daily from the suspended chair.

For more than a decade Morritt's career flourished. This success arose from his performing skills (although his style struck some as overly energetic and fast-paced). But it was also due to his accomplishments as an inventor—a creator of large-scale illusions. These illusions were devised and built in his basement workshop. Among them were the Turkish Delight (four Turkish women appear out of nowhere)— first performed during a tour of Australia in 1897—and the Convict's Escape (a prisoner vanishes from a cage within a cage). Most of Morritt's illusions depended on the use of mirrors, which were his specialty. Indeed, he seems to have been obsessed with mirrors.

But Charles Morritt had succeeded professionally despite a drinking problem. And as his alcoholism worsened, his work—and personal life—suffered. Lillian left him. He was reduced to performing in provincial music halls and dime museums. And when his associates in London had not seen him in years, the rumor circulated that he was dead.

•

When Morritt left Maskelyne's company, his place was taken by David Devant. Devant was young and talented; had an engaging personality; and eventually became Britain's most popular magician. And one day in 1912, he was visiting Hexham, a town in northern England. Told that a magician was appearing at a local theatre, he went over to see who it was. And he found this sign on a small, storefront theatre:

PROFESSOR CHARLES MORRITT PRESENTS
THE DISAPPEARING DONKEY

Devant could scarcely believe his eyes; for he thought Charles Morritt was dead. He knocked on the door. Morritt answered, recognized Devant, smiled broadly, and welcomed him inside.

They talked about old times. And Morritt described

what he had been doing in recent years: managing theatres and occasionally performing. Last year in Glasgow, he said, his Man in a Trance act had drawn a sizeable audience.

Then he offered to demonstrate The Disappearing Donkey. Devant was eager to see it and took a seat in the empty theatre. Morritt went off to prepare.

When the curtain opened, a donkey and a clown were revealed, and a large cabinet. The cabinet was raised up on legs. It had two doors at the front, which were shut. A ramp led up to a side door.

Morritt came out with a hoop covered with stretched fabric. He hung it behind the cabinet. Then he opened the front doors and a curtain at the rear of the cabinet (which had no rear wall). This allowed Devant to see through the cabinet. Visible were the hoop and the back portion of the stage. Having displayed its interior, Morritt closed up the cabinet.

The clown now led the donkey up the ramp. He had to pull forcefully on the reins; for the beast resisted, kicking and stomping. Morritt was urging it on with a rider's crop. Finally, the donkey was inside the cabinet—still stomping noisily. The clown leapt out; and Morritt closed the side door.

Suddenly, there was silence. The donkey was no longer stomping.

"Open it up!" commanded Morritt.

The clown flung open the front doors. And the donkey was gone—was nowhere to be seen! The cabinet was empty (or so it seemed). The clown went around and pulled aside the curtain. Devant could see straight through to the hoop and the back of the stage.

He applauded; and the applause echoed in the empty theatre. When Morritt came down from the stage, Devant praised the illusion. And he was thinking, he told Morritt, about how it might play in London.

Charles Morritt was soon back in London—hired by Devant to perform the donkey illusion. He was accompanied by a woman named Bessie, his new assistant and companion. The Disappearing Donkey was an immediate hit; and for the next three years Morritt performed it and other illusions at St. George's Hall. He also worked with Devant, and with Houdini, in the creation of illusions.

But again he grew restless. And in 1915 he left Devant's company, to be featured in a show at the Royal Polytechnic. His new illusion was Tally Ho!, in which an entire hunting party—a woman on a horse, two huntsmen, and a hound— emerge from an empty cabinet. But the show was a failure and closed after a few months. Disillusioned with London, Morritt resumed his itinerant ways. He and Bessie roamed from town to town, performing in small theatres. They billed themselves as Morritt the Mystery Man and Madame Beulah the Lightning Calculator. For a while he managed a dance hall in Bristol. The years went by.

Then, in October 1927, Morritt was arrested and charged with having deceived an audience!

It involved his Man in a Trance act, an old standby in which an accomplice pretends to be in a trance. Morritt was appearing at a theatre in Halifax, on the same bill as a movie. He had previously recruited, and trained as an accomplice, a pedlar known as Billy Fish. As arranged, Billy volunteered from the audience, came on stage, and pretended to be hypnotized. Then he climbed into a coffin and lay there as if in a trance.

For a week Halifaxians viewed him, as Morritt expounded on the mysteries of hypnotism. Supposedly, Billy was in a deep trance. In reality, when not on display, he was eating, drinking, and smoking in a room beneath the theatre. Finally, Morritt "woke" him in front of a packed house, and took up a collection for Billy and his family.

But the police learned that the two men had been in collusion; that the trance had been fake; and that Morritt had pocketed half of the collection. They charged him with obtaining money under false pretenses. A trial date was set; but the trial was delayed when Morritt had to be hospitalized. Magicians in London raised money to cover his legal and medical bills.

In the end the charges were dropped. But the episode left Charles Morritt broken in body and spirit; and he never again performed. He and Bessie settled in a seaside resort. There he began to write an autobiography (the manuscript has been lost); while Bessie, in a booth on the promenade, told fortunes.

●

For nearly a century The Disappearing Donkey baffled magicians. The illusion involved mirrors—that they knew; for Morritt had specialized in optical trickery. But how exactly had mirrors been used? What was the role of the hoop? And a further mystery concerned the donkey itself. How had so stubborn a creature been induced to cooperate and disappear?

Donkeys are notoriously intractable; and true to form, Morritt's had resisted being led into the cabinet. It had kicked and stomped; and only with a sustained effort were they able to get it up the ramp and through the side door. Once inside the cabinet, it had continued to stomp loudly. Yet no sooner had the door been closed than the donkey fell silent. Suddenly, it had become compliant (or had indeed vanished into thin air). This abrupt change only deepened the mystery.

But the puzzle was finally solved—by Jim Steinmeyer, author of *Hiding the Elephant* (published in 2003 and my main source for information about Morritt). A designer of stage illusions, Steinmeyer had for years been trying to figure out The Disappearing Donkey. Devant too had performed it, and had left behind notes, with stage directions. Steinmeyer read and re-read these notes. Yet the secret eluded him. The breakthrough came when a magician-friend studied the illusion—and saw the significance of the clown.

Clowns, he reminded Steinmeyer, were used by magicians for the purpose of "doubling." Two persons in identical clown costumes were interchangeable. Thus, one could secretly take the other's place—the sort of substitution that played a key role in some illusions (and which had first been employed by Servais Le Roy). So why had a clown—and not a trainer—led the donkey into the cabinet? Because *two* clowns had somehow been involved in the illusion.

Steinmeyer also learned of an incident that had taken place at St. George's Hall. He came across this account of it, written by Maskelyne's grandson:

> We were presenting a trick with a donkey, but the donkey disappeared before its time. An agitated magician came running up. "My donkey's disappeared!" he gasped. "Some fool's left the door open at the back, and the damned beast has vanished. We're due to go on in five minutes. What shall we do?"
>
> I hastily said a word to the stage-manager and, assisted by two clowns in full make-up, raced out into Langham Place to try to trace the lost quadruped. I was presently joined by no fewer than five policemen, and we presently ran him to ground nearly half a mile away.... The donkey, escorted back to the theatre by the five constables, two clowns and myself, arrived in time to be included as the penultimate turn of the evening.

Here was evidence that a pair of clowns had been involved. And that insight led Steinmeyer to a solution of the puzzle. What follows is his reconstruction of The Disappearing Donkey—how he believes the illusion must have been effected.

The initial clown (the one that led the donkey up the ramp) was not a performer, says Steinmeyer. Rather, he was the donkey's trainer—someone who knew how to manage it. Yet unaccountably, he had pulled the donkey forward by its reins, causing it to kick and stomp. Any trainer would have known to walk alongside the donkey and cajole it. Therefore, Steinmeyer concluded, the trainer must have *wanted* it to protest noisily.

Meanwhile, a second clown had hidden himself in the cabinet. Once the donkey and trainer were inside, this double jumped out. Thus, the trainer—unbeknownst to the audience—remained inside the cabinet. Why? Because he was needed there to manage the donkey.

Immediately, with soothing words he silenced the donkey —to make it seem as if it had vanished. And he did more than silence the donkey. For he quickly maneuvered it into its hiding place.

This hiding place was an ingenious affair. Attached to the rear of the cabinet was a "load space"—a platform or container just large enough to hold the donkey and trainer. In front of the load space, shielding it from view, was a mirror. The mirror was hinged, and could be raised and lowered like a clamshell. It was controlled from beneath the stage, via ropes that ran through the legs of the cabinet.

Upon entering the cabinet, the trainer had maneuvered the donkey into the load space. Squeezing in alongside it, he signaled for the mirror—which had been raised to admit them—to be lowered into position.

Morritt's expertise with optics was the key to what followed. The mirror was precisely positioned and angled at 45 degrees. So when the front doors were opened and the curtain at the rear was pulled aside, an illusion greeted the eye. The audience thought it was seeing straight through the cabinet and viewing the hoop. In fact, it was seeing only the upper half of the hoop. *What seemed to be the lower half was merely a reflection of the upper half.* Behind that reflection—behind the mirror—was the donkey.

To test his theory, Steinmeyer decided to perform The Disappearing Donkey. He constructed the cabinet; had a mirror made; and hired a donkey. And in the fall of 1995, at the Conference on Magic History in Los Angeles, he performed the illusion before an audience of magicians. It had been nearly a century since its last performance.

On a ballroom stage Steinmeyer made the donkey disappear; and his fellow magicians applauded enthusiastically. He acknowledged their applause. And although seen by no one, the ghost of Charles Morritt—clad in evening dress and somewhat tipsy—stood beside him and bowed.

C. W. Starr

C.W. STARR (*c.* 1850–?) WAS AN ITINERANT MAGICIAN, who traveled from town to town in New York state. Assisted by his wife Maud, he would perform at the local opera house. Their act was a modest one. But Starr had hopes of enhancing it, with new tricks. And he wrote this letter to a Chicago magic dealer:

Clarence Centre, N.Y.
November 5th, 1887

Dear Sir:

Your advertisement is before me. I am very anxious to know what *Buatier's Cocoon* and the "*Original Egyptian Black Art*" mean, as they are both something that I have never either seen or heard of until reading your "ad." I am giving little shows in little towns, and am making a *little, very little money.* But am not having to walk [i.e., skip out on a hotel bill], or leave any baggage for debts. I even can spare a little money, a *very little money*, to pay for anything that would have a tendency to induce more people to patronize me. I mix magic tricks, spiritualistic tricks and idiotic expressions all together, and deal the mixture out to the eager, grasping few who pay me ten cents for the privilege of being humbugged. So, if you can add anything to this mixture to make it more palatable to my patrons, just sit down and tell me about what you have, how much it will cost me to get it, when I can get it, etc.

For a few years back, many professionals, and several amateurs I have met in the rural districts that have been blessed with my "90 laughs in 90 minutes," have all and each added their mites to my conglomeration; that is to say, I have bought and paid the cash for several of their cheapest tricks....

I am not a rival of Heller, nor Keller, nor no other feller of any magnitude. I am a poor little country showman, that has neither the big head nor big pocket book; but I know I am a small fish and I stay in the small streams and bask in the sunshine with the other little minnies, and am enjoying life. I don't owe anybody and nobody owes me. I do not want to be tedious but I make these explanations, so that if you make apparatus only for such men as Herrmann, Kellar and the great magicians, you will not waste any time on me at present. I hope to be great some day, but that day with me has not arrived. The most I ever paid for a trick in my life was ten dollars, but I would like to buy five more at the same price today, if I could get as good ones as the one I mention. It is an apparatus for lifting tables, chairs, stools, and other articles of furniture, à la spiritualism.

I want your unrivaled catalogue, and, rather than have you make fun of my little descriptive bill, I will enclose you ten cents for the catalogue and request you to send it by return mail, as I am *en route*, and only stay in a village long enough to work up my own advertising, give my show, and pull out for another town. I am my own advance agent, programmer, business manager, treasurer, property man, door-keeper, usher, stage hand, carpenter, scene shifter, scenic artist, actor, lecturer, humbugger, and sheriff dodger. I am all combined in one.

If you think it worth while to send me one of your catalogues for my ten cents, I would be glad to get it; if not, keep the ten cents anyway to pay for reading this long letter.

Very respectfully yours,
C. W. STARR

The letter is quoted in *Leaves from Conjurers' Scrap Books* (1891) by Hardin J. Burlingame, who describes Starr as "quite well known throughout the small towns of the East." Yet Starr was not always welcome in those towns. As an itinerant showman—a roving magician—a humbugger!—he occasionally roused the suspicion of local authorities.

Hence, among the many hats that he describes himself as wearing was that of sheriff dodger.

But the humbugger had another vocation—one in which he *exposed* humbuggery. For Starr was also a lecturer, on the deceitful practices of fake mediums. His lectures featured demonstrations of those practices and were well-attended. "Prof. C.W. Starr's novel entertainment entitled 'A Night with the Spirits' was given in Becker & Campbell Hall Friday night, to a large audience," reported the *Oswego Morning Express*. And this notice appeared in the *Rushford Spectator*:

STARR COMING.

Prof. C.W. Starr will deliver a course of five illustrated lectures in the Academy Hall in this village…upon the subject of Spiritualism. Prof. Starr illustrates his lectures with all of the leading phenomena incident to the craze…. he is thoroughly acquainted with all of their artifices for deceiving the public, and he presents the most exciting of their mysteries in such a pleasing style as to keep his audience delighted from the opening to the close.

Like Houdini a half-century later, Starr exposed those deceptions and their perpetrators. He demonstrated the techniques used by mediums to "communicate" with the dead and deceive the credulous. And it was during the course of his lecturing that he met with, and exposed, that most notorious of mediums, Henry Slade.

In November 1883 he and Slade met in Malone, a town in upstate New York, near the Canadian border. Starr was using an assumed name and did not reveal his true identity until the end. A detailed account of their encounter appeared in the *Franklin Gazette*, a weekly published in Malone. Newly discovered, that account offers an intimate view of Slade at work, and is reproduced here in its entirety:

SPIRITS!

DR. HENRY SLADE INTERVIEWED BY PROF. C. W. STARR.

THE MOST FORMIDABLE ENEMY THE SPIRITUALISTIC MEDIUMS HAVE EVER HAD TO CONTEND WITH.

ANOTHER DIAMOND IN PROF. STARR'S ALREADY GORGEOUS CROWN OF GLORY.

For some two years past Modern Spiritualism has been attracting considerable attention in Malone. Many of our prominent and leading business men, men of high standing in the community, have been investigating with quite a degree of interest its claims to bring back the dead. If this interest was simply confined to the lesser intelligent portions of society we would not feel so much inclined to devote so much of our space to this article; but since this gigantic humbug has grown to such proportions as to excite the curiosity and patronage of so many of our influential citizens, it becomes our duty to do all we can to thwart its operations.

When we take into consideration that this monster bugbear has succeeded in attracting the attention of and so completely carrying away the confidence the world once had in such valuable members of society as Joseph Cook, Robert Dale Owen, Judge Edmunds, Judge Welch, Judge Colgrove, Prof. Kiddle, Judge Hare, Prof. Wm. Crookes, F. R. S. [Fellow of the Royal Society], Prof. Zoellner, and many others among the world's eminent scholars—might be if they had not been led astray by it—perhaps we can excuse the excitement that at present prevails in Malone over the wonderful phenomena witnessed at the seances recently held at the house of one of our citizens through the mediumship of modern spiritualism's greatest medium, Dr. Henry Slade, of New York city.

About three weeks ago this Dr. Slade came to our enterprising little village and opened up his spiritualist seances, charging therefore $3.00 a single ticket to each seance. That he met with abundant success is evident, as even in these days, so near an election, when politics usually swallow up all other topics of conversation, you can hardly remain in any group of men five minutes without hearing the Doctor and his seances discussed.

After putting in a week of unlimited success, he returned to his home in New York to remain a few days, and then returned.

On Thursday and Friday evenings of last week he gave talks upon his experiences from his early advent as a medium up to the present time and telling of his conquests among the scholars of the Old World, during his travels through England, France, Germany and Russia, and asserting his honest, and his utter disdain of deceit, and his determination to continue in his work and earnestly appealed to all to "investigate," but not to question his honesty for a moment, and to treat him as though we had perfect confidence in his integrity and the results at his seances would be the more astonishing. Last Thursday evening Prof. Starr, who was at that time holding a course of lectures at Colton, St. Lawrence Co., was notified that Dr. Slade was here, and he left Colton early the next morning for this place, arriving here on the 6 o'clock train, in time to hear Dr. Slade's last lecture. Prof. Starr, knowing that his name is to all spirit mediums what the name of Allen Pinkerton is to all horse thieves, a dread and a terror, wisely concealed his name and registered at the Ferguson House as George Waters, of New York city. After the close of Slade's lecture Friday night, Prof. Starr, under the name of Geo. Waters, and assuming the business of a traveling photographer, approached Dr. Slade, and asked when he could have a seance. The doctor said, "Some time tomorrow." So Mr. Waters went to bed, and next morning the doctor appointed one o'clock as the time, and requested Mr. Waters to purchase a couple of slates at the book store, as he, the doctor, had none.

Mr. Waters bought six slates instead of two, took them to his hotel room and put a private mark in three different places on each of the six slates, and with them under his arm, arrived at the place where the seance was to be held promptly at one o'clock. The gentleman of the house met him at the door and ushered him into the lower back parlor, where Slade was sitting. After a moment or two's common conversation, the doctor rising to his feet, smilingly said, "Well, we will go—up into the morgue," and Mr. ———, in a jesting manner remarked, "Well, good bye; we may never see you again," to which Waters replied: "Good bye, sir; I'm well armed for the conflict."

Upon entering the upper front bed-chamber, or seance room, Mr. Waters was invited to be seated at a what to all appearance, seemed to be a common kitchen table with raised leaves, when Dr. Slade reached out his hands for the slates, but Mr. Waters, holding tight to them, said:

"Doctor, I have been told that I would be allowed the privilege of doing all of the handling of the slates myself—that they would never pass out of my hands. If you will grant me that privilege, I wish you would—"

(Seeming much provoked)—"Why!" said the doctor, "that is a mistake; you have been misinformed. Why, what would be the use of you coming to me, if you could get communications without my handling the slates?"

"That's so," said Mr. Waters, taking in the situation at a glance. "I beg your pardon for suggesting I should allow you to do that, for you understand your business better than I do, of course, and during the balance of the seance I shall do just as you say."

Slade then took the slates and washed each one off carefully with a wet sponge, remarking that he was sorry Waters had procured slates with a wire binding, as they were not so good, but he would try them. He then took one slate in his right hand and after dropping a bit of pencil upon it, reached it under the table—out of sight, entirely—and from the direction of his arm, Mr. Waters thought he laid it upon his, Slade's knees. It remained there just about long enough for the doctor to write upon it, with his concealed right hand, about half-a-dozen words. Mr. Waters heard what he thought was writing on the slate while the slate was under the table, out of sight; but he said nothing, but watched closely the movement of the part of Slade's arm that was exposed to view, as it also moved perceptibly, enough to still further convince Mr. Waters that the slate pencil that made the noise was moved by the hand that was attached to that arm. The slate was then, after the noise of the writing had ceased, raised to near the under side of the table-top, and held with a little of one end of it in sight. The doctor then asked, "Will the spirits be able to use these slates?" when a louder scratching noise was then heard, that did not sound so much like a slate pencil as it did like a finger nail.

The slate was drawn forth and a few scrawly marks were found to be on the top side of the slate, that the doctor said meant "We will try," and a signature that he informed Mr. Waters meant "W. W." and asked Waters if he had any relative that was dead that W. W. would stand for the name of. Upon receiving a negative answer, he said, "We'll try again."

The same performance of putting another slate under the table, with all the above suspicious sounds and movement, was gone through with and the slate removed when lo and behold, it contained the entreating message in what appeared to be more like Chinese writing than anything else, that the doctor interpreted to mean "do not doubt" signed, "J. W." Again the Dr. asked the question, "Have you any relative there (meaning on the other side) that 'J. W.' would stand for, or may be that's 'F. W.' any John Waters or Frank, or anything like that?"

Answer. "No, sir; but I had an Uncle Joe." "Oh!" said the Dr., "well that's him, yes, I see the 'J' stands for 'Joe.'"

Mr. Waters pretended to be very much surprised. And still there's more to follow. While the doctor was insisting upon it that this communication was of vast importance, and asked with great emphasis, "How could you doubt such a wonderful evidence?"

The doctor drew himself closer to the table and presently Mr. Waters felt something touching him on the right side of the right knee, which felt to him very much as though the doctor was kicking him with the top of his slipper. At the same time the doctor started up and exclaimed excitedly, "There! look there! did you see that? Why—"

Waters—"No, where?" feigning equal excitement. "But I felt it."

Doctor—"Felt what?"

Waters—"Something struck me on," apparently almost out of breath, "on my leg, on the opposite side from you." And as he said it, he sprang from his seat, and could not be induced by the doctor to resume his seat at the table, until he had first looked under the bed and behind all the furniture in the room, to see if someone was not concealed in the room. After satisfying himself that no one was or could get into the room, Mr. Waters still pretending timidity, took his seat, which he had no sooner done, than a large, heavy office chair, which stood on the opposite side of the table, jumped about a foot away from where it was standing, and although, the doctor was sitting in reach of it with his foot and [could have] kicked violently with it in the direction of the chair. Mr. Waters declared it to be wonderful and asked the doctor, "What on earth do you supposed jerked that chair so violently?"

Doctor—"Spirits, my dear, sir. I declare, we are having a splendid seance today."

Waters—"Is it possible, spirits?"

Doctor—"Yes, indeed. What else could it be? What else could have such power?"

Waters—"That's so. It beat the Jews; don't it, doctor."

Doctor—"Why, I should say so!"

He then grabbed a slate and pencil, excitedly: "This is Mr. Davis's spirit that is controlling me now, he is writing, see! with my hand." And as Mr. Waters leaned forward to see, Slade said, "Sit still! Sit still; don't break the circuit!" so all Waters could see was that the doctor was holding the slate above the table and, while doing so, was writing a slate full of a communication, which he claimed he was doing with no volition of his own, but that the spirit of a Mr. Davis was doing the writing with his, the doctor's, hand. After the slate was written full, instead of showing the writing to Mr. Waters, Slade still kept the writing out of sight, but pretended to read it aloud. What he read was this:

"Mr. Davis says. 'Mr. Waters is a medium, not fully developed, but is rapidly becoming so. Very soon powerful manifestations will take place in his presence and through his organism he will not be able to produce *independent slate-writing,* but many other tests equally as convincing—even more convincing. Proceed with your investigation and become fully developed.'"

Although Mr. Waters does not claim to be proof against flattery, this bit of a compliment did not serve to produce its desired effect—to draw Mr. Waters' attention from the fact that Slade kept the side of the slate that contained the writing away from Waters, and then put the slate down into his, Slade's, own lap, written side down, and deliberately took a wet sponge and washed over the top of the slate—the side upon which there was no writing at all—and then as coolly announced that he would put that clean slate aside now and try another, and in putting it aside he put it away over on the other side of the table out of Mr. Waters' reach. But after trying another with unsatisfactory results, he said, "I guess I'll have to take that other slate again; it seems to be the best."

It will be remembered by the reader that this one that he now takes up, that he says seems to be the best, has already one side full of writing, but which the doctor calls "this clean slate that I just now washed," and he still keeps concealed, the side containing the written message, from Waters' eyes, and places the two slates together with the side already containing the communication on the inside, and the while glibly talking at random, he tries, holding the slates in one position and another, until he finally gets it near his victim's shoulder, and the finger-nail scratching noise is again heard, which the doctor says is the pencil on the inside writing. Presently a noise that sounded as though he was tapping on the under side of the slate with his finger nail is heard, and he said: "They are rapping, that is a sign they are done." He then opened the slates and there appeared upon the slate a long communication, as follows:

"My dear boy, why do you doubt this when the facts are so plain?" Just here Mr. Waters thought, and could hardly refrain from saying, "Yes not only the facts but the bottom facts are plainer to me than you dream of!" But the communication further read: "Yes, I am your Uncle Joe, and am often with you. Go on in your investigation, and learn wisdom. I am truly your uncle, Joe W."

"Well! Well! Well!" exclaimed Waters with all the forced excitement he could muster, both in voice and action. "This takes the cake. If that don't beat anything I ever saw. Well! Well! Doctor, what did that writing?"

"Your Uncle Joe Waters' spirit, of course."

"Doctor, do you mean to tell me that my Uncle Joe Waters wrote that to me?"

"Most certainly I do. What else could it have been?"

He then picked up another slate, held it under the table a moment, drew it forth, and there were the words written upon it, "Good bye."

This closed the seance. Mr. Waters paid the doctor $3.00, the price of the seance, and they adjourned to the lower parlor, where Mr. ——— was still sitting reading. As they entered the room, Mr. ——— said, "Well, you are back again alive. How were you satisfied?"

"Perfectly," said Waters. "I wouldn't have missed it for ten times the amount. I'm coming again."

The doctor, after paying Mr. Waters a high compliment as being a shrewd but honest man, addressing his remarks to Mr. ———, invited Mr. Waters to come again tomorrow and try another seance. "But," said the doctor to Mr. ———, "however, we could hardly expect to have a better one, for it was one of the best seances I've held here."

After again assuring the doctor of his entire satisfaction with the results of the seance and of the high value the slate communication from his dear Uncle Joe Waters was to him, Mr. Waters bid the doctor an affectionate farewell and left with the promise to return next day.

Prof. Starr then came right down street and contracted for the opera house, and began to make arrangements for a course of five lectures upon the subject of Spiritualism, in which he will show that what is known as Modern Spiritualism is simply one gigantic system of deceit and the continuation, under another name, of the business of obtaining money by soothsaying, necromancy, etc., that is spoken of in the scriptures. He will show the analogy between the two, and show up the false claims of all the leading mediums in the United States, including their king of impostors, the great Dr. Henry Slade, who has been all around the world turning the heads of those to whom the Bible says "God shall send strong delusions." (II Thes. chap. ii; 9th to 12th verses inclusive)

Prof. Starr will devote a portion of one of the five evenings to giving a seance *à la* Dr. Slade—that is, do just what Dr. Slade does at his seances, and explain and expose it so clearly that all can understand and know just exactly how it is done. And Prof. Starr offers a challenge of $500 to Dr. Slade, or any other medium on earth that will meet him and give any spirit test twice in his presence, and under circumstances which preclude all possibility of deception, that he, Starr, can not do and show by positive and indisputable proof that spirits of the dead have nothing to do with it.

Now this is business, and Prof. Starr deserves the gratitude of the whole world for the unflinching stand he takes against this monster evil, and for the thorough and complete, and satisfactory expose he gives of the mysteries of the spiritual circle. He is a man of almost superhuman ability to detect even the slightest movement of any part of the medium's body or face, and to trace the cause of the movement. He is personally acquainted with nearly every prominent spirit medium in the world; has caught a great many of them in their swindling operations, and those who had secrets he could not see through he has swapped tricks with, so that he stands today able and ready to do anything that actually takes place at any spiritual seance in the world and explain it satisfactorily.

Prof. Starr does not advertise to do all that he is told by others that they have seen done. This could not be expected of him, for a great many stories have been told to him by honest, candid gentlemen, about things that they say they have seen done at spiritual seances, that, although they are perfectly sincere in their assertions, distance lends such enchantment to the view that they often, unintentionally, make misstatements, yet he stands fearlessly to the front with the ability to do all that actually does take place at any spiritual seance in America.

Sunday afternoon at three o'clock, Prof. Starr, still under the name of Waters, accompanied by Sheriff Stockwell, seated themselves at the doctor's table, and the spirits commenced to rap. One or two partially successful attempts were made to get slate communications, and the doctor raised his left leg underneath the table and was preparing to give the Sheriff a "spirit touch," when Waters (Prof. Starr) detecting the movement, raised his leg also and caught and held the doctor's leg for a moment, but he struggled loose, and, as an excuse for having his leg so out of place, claimed that the spirits got into his leg and complained of the terrible pains he suffered in it.

This brought the seance to an abrupt close. The sheriff left, but Waters (Prof. Starr) remained and had quite a talk with the doctor all alone. He told the doctor he had detected him in each trick, when the doctor said, "Is that so? How? Show me how I did it?"

Waters (Prof. Starr) then produced a communication for the doctor and explained how he detected him in each of the others. The doctor begged of him not to reveal the secret and promised to come around to the hotel and see Waters (Starr) in the morning (Monday).

Dr. Slade kept his agreement to call Monday morning, when Prof. Starr then revealed his true name and business to the doctor and read him a formal challenge to meet him here next week.

The doctor then, after an unsuccessful attempt to induce Prof. Starr not to expose him here, said: "I don't know whether it will be possible for me to be present or not. I will see. I will try to be back by next Sunday, or at least before you get through here." Whether the doctor gets back or not, Prof. Starr will give a course of lectures and seances in the Opera House next week, showing up Modern Spiritualism to be the deepest laid plot for thieves to pick honest men's pockets with in existence. And we predict larger audiences than were ever before in Lawrence Opera House, and if Prof. Starr succeeds in annihilating the effects of this scourge that has broken out among us, the village authorities should give him some token of respect worthy of his work.

Dr. Slade left here last Monday morning on the ten o'clock train for Potsdam.

Prof. Starr has been offered the pulpit of the Methodist

church, which is the largest audience room in the village, and will deliver an address, or sermon on the subject of "Spiritualism," next Sabbath evening at the usual hour for services.

●

From dodging sheriffs to being offered a pulpit, C. W. Starr experienced the vicissitudes that have so often marked the life of a conjurer.

Also available from Top Hat Press:

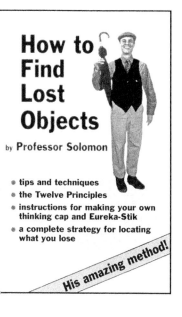

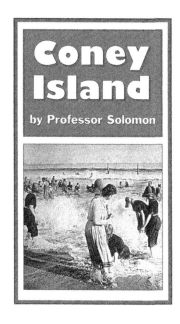

Printed in Great Britain
by Amazon

39962464R00099